MARY: DISCIPLE & MOTHER

MARY: DISCIPLE & MOTHER

Fr Ken Barker MGL

Connor Court Publishing

Published in 2020 by Connor Court Publishing Pty Ltd
Copyright © Fr Ken Barker 2020

All rights reserved. No part of this book may be reproduced or transmitted in any form or by any means, electronic or mechanical, including photocopying, recording or by any information storage and retrieval system, without prior permission in writing from the publisher.

Connor Court Publishing Pty Ltd
PO Box 7257
Redland Bay QLD 4165

sales@connorcourt.com
www.connorcourtpublishing.com.au
Phone 0497 900 685

ISBN: 9781 922 449 023

Imprimatur
Most Rev Christopher Prowse DD STD
Archbishop of Canberra and Goulburn

Front Cover Design: Br Lawrence Yuen MLG
Printed in Australia

CONTENTS

FOREWORD	7
INTRODUCTION	9
PART I MARY AS DISCIPLE	13
1. The Wonder of Grace	15
2. Courageous Faith	21
3. Boundless Trust	26
4. Surrender to the Lord	32
5. Contemplative of Heart	46
PART II MARY AS OUR MOTHER	57
6. Woman, Behold your Son!	59
7. Mother of the Church	70
8. Mother who intercedes for us	79
PART III MARY AND THE HOLY SPIRIT	91
9. Mary and Pentecost	93
10. Mary as Charismatic	108
11. Healing and Miracles	119
12. Mother of Evangelisation	129
ENTRUSTMENT TO MARY	141
ENDNOTES	145

I wish to thank Selina Hasham for casting her eye over the text and making valuable suggestions. Also thanks to Br Lawrence Yuen MGL for the artwork on the front page. As always I am grateful to my MGL brothers and sisters who continue to inspire me. I dedicate the book to my dear mother, who went to the Lord in 2014, and was always a tender and faithful presence in my life.

FOREWORD

Fr. Ken Barker MGL has written yet another wonderful book – this time titled: MARY, DISCIPLE AND MOTHER.

In this latest book, Fr Barker demonstrates a talent for harmonising together two seemingly very diverse dimensions of our Catholic popular piety: traditional Catholic devotional teaching on Mary, the Mother of God, and Charismatic spirituality.

He does this by an extended meditation on two key words, Disciple and Mother.

As a disciple, our faith proclaims that Mary is always first among the faithful. She is a kind of first Christian disciple.

As the first missionary disciple, Fr Barker examines her as "full of grace". Mary would be the first to proclaim this in the Magnificat as a sheer gift of God's love. Mary surrenders everything in trust to the Lord with a contemplative heart.

Fr Barker observes that this contemplative dimension is of great importance in the Gospels which "are more eloquent about the silence of Mary than about anything she says". He expresses this eloquently when he observes that Mary "loved to be alone with God". He draws out implications for Mary as disciple for us all.

In regard to Mary as Mother, he draws from the Hans Urs von Balthasar theological insight of the Marian dimension of the Church. Recent Popes have stressed this in their writings. Teachings of Pope Francis "that the Church of all the baptised is feminine. The Church is a mother" are reflected upon by Fr Barker at length.

Perhaps the most original material in this easy to read book concerns the statement by Fr Barker that "Mary is the first charismatic". As he explains very personally, Fr Barker re-discovered his deep devotion to Mary via his participation in Charismatic Renewal. His experiences would surely assist us all to move away from elements of sentimentality to a renewed biblically based devotion of Mary as charismatic.

This deeply personal book is the fruit of Fr Barker's intense prayer life. At times, it is almost as if we are eavesdropping on his deepest spiritual thoughts. For this we are truly grateful and brought closer to Mary, who always points out Jesus to us alive in the Church.

It is extraordinary how devotion to Mary always brings us together in Christ. This has always happened in our Christian history. It is happening afresh today as well. I have been staggered, for example, how reference to Mary is so helpful in inter-religious dialogue and not simply dialogue among Christians. She is the mother and disciple to all of us!

In his book Fr Barker has helped us to understand the reasons for this. May we all grow closer to Jesus by reading this prayerful book as a real assistance to our own prayer life.

Archbishop Christopher Prowse
Catholic Archbishop of Canberra Goulburn.

INTRODUCTION

In writing this book, I am inviting you to enter into deeper personal communion with the Blessed Virgin Mary as our model disciple and as our loving Mother. Many people begin the deeper spiritual journey with scant reference to Mary. I was one of those. As a young priest, after experiencing a new infilling of the Holy Spirit, I found the centrality of Jesus in my life in a fresh and exciting way. I could profess, "Jesus is Lord!" with a conviction and vigour that previously I had lacked. With this newfound love for Jesus, the earlier somewhat sentimental devotions to Mary seemed to be superceded and could be set aside. The new blinding revelation of the Risen Jesus as my Saviour and Lord was all-encompassing and any traditional devotions lost their relevance and disappeared into the background.

With this new revelation, I did not in any way deny the great dogmas of the Blessed Virgin Mary. To the contrary, I would have defended them to death. But they remained somewhat cerebral affirmations of faith, to be upheld, but with little impact on my interior journey. They were simply part of the Catholic package. In truth, I was lacking any real experience of a close relationship with Mary.

After a couple of years of this new Pentecost experience it began to dawn on me that Mary's centrality to the saving mystery of Christ was not accidental. If I wanted to be authentically a follower of Jesus, this could not be neglected. I began to feel my poverty. I did not feel complete having the teaching of Mary as abstract ideas in my mind. The Holy Spirit was opening my heart to seek an authentic relationship with Mary. So before a grotto of the Blessed Virgin I asked Jesus to show me his Mother. Everything changed from that moment.

Usually Catholics will ask the Blessed Virgin to take them to Jesus. My experience was in the reverse. I begged her Son to introduce me to Mary in a personal way. If any reader feels like I did, needing a revelation of Mary's role in your life, I suggest you do the same. I can assure you it works. After all, Jesus gave his Mother to John the Beloved, and hence to all his disciples, and he eagerly wants to give her to anyone who is open to receiving the gift.

On the other hand, I am aware that some people who pick up this book may already feel they have a strong relationship with the Blessed Virgin Mary. Praise God for that! I trust you will find the reflections here helpful for you to deepen in your love for her. You will notice that I have tried to stay away from some of the excesses of devotion that have been handed down as unnecessary accretions in the broad Catholic tradition. I have instead taken the lead from Pope Paul VI's Apostolic Exhortation, *Marialis Cultus*.[1] The Pope enumerates four criteria for a genuine Marian spirituality.

a) Biblical – that it is truly grounded in the Scriptural revelation. I have focussed particularly on the way the four gospel writers have presented Mary.

b) Liturgical- that it is in harmony with the official worship of the Church, in keeping with the dictum, *"lex orandi, lex credendi"* i.e. the way we pray expresses the way we believe.

c) Ecumenical – that it avoids any exaggerations that would mislead other Christians about the true doctrine of the Catholic Church. That it would be appealing to other Christians in such a way that our love for Mary will in time "become a path and a rallying point for all who believe in Christ."[2]

d) Contemporary – that it presents Mary as a model for modern women, not according to a type of sentimentality and piosity akin to a previous age but as a positive, strong, vigorous, courageous and responsible woman.

So many inspiring works on Mary have already been written in the post-Vatican II era. I cannot expect to say anything that is radically new. However, I trust this is a worthwhile exercise to share with you what I find most attractive about the Blessed Mother and why I have entrusted myself to her loving protection and care.

I am not a wide-eyed Marian enthusiast with various scapulars and medals around my neck and a different pair of rosary beads for every day and a pocket full of miraculous medals to distribute at the drop of a hat. I *do* have a scapular, I *do* pray the rosary every day, and I believe strongly in the power of the miraculous medal. But these devotional aids are not my badge, as if I needed these accessories to be authentic. Rather, my Marian spirituality is a quiet, somewhat hidden, but very real, warm, mother-son relationship that is somewhat difficult to define.

It is something like the relationship I had with my earthly mother, who died in 2014. She had always been a quiet, background figure in my priestly journey, but nevertheless a vital personal support with unconditional love. She was also a tenacious supporter of the Missionaries of God's Love, to which I belong. I suggest that Jesus experienced his mother something like that in his earthly journey, but of course free of all the usual imperfections of earthly mothers. That is how I experience Mary in my life also.

The Gospels are more eloquent about the silence of Mary than about anything she says. She in no way pushes herself forward to gain attention. Rather, her attitude is always to point towards Jesus, as at Cana, with the unforgettable words, "Do whatever he tells you" (Jn 2:5). Like John the Baptist, and more so, Mary can say of her Son, "He must increase, and I must decrease" (Jn 3:30). Her humble, quiet presence in the background speaks loudly of her holiness as we shall see in the pages to come. She does not want us to exalt her for her own sake, but rather that through her we exalt her Son. Yet, to depict Mary as having nothing important to say would not be true to

Scriptural revelation. Likewise, to imagine her as simply passive under God's grace, having no real challenges in life once she gave her initial "yes" to God's plan, would not be true to reality.

The book is divided into three main parts. The first reflects upon Mary as the first disciple, and hence the model for all discipleship. The second shows how Mary is our tender, loving mother. Each of us is called into a unique and unrepeatable loving relationship with her, as a child to a mother. We are to entrust ourselves into her loving care. Mary has a big family, but, because she abides totally in Christ, she manages to be mother of us all. She is also Mother of the Church. She is the exemplar for the Church, inspiring us to deeper faith, hope and love. The third part reflects on Mary as filled with the Holy Spirit and hence profoundly charismatic. Then it describes how, as Mother of the Church, she cooperates with the Spirit in the rebirthing of the Church throughout history.

PART I

MARY AS DISCIPLE

1

THE WONDER OF GRACE

The story in Luke's gospel of the Angel Gabriel coming to Mary proclaims powerfully the wonder of God's grace. Everything happens because of God's gracious initiative. Later when Mary is with Elizabeth, she sums up the whole experience in a beautiful song of praise, which we call the Magnificat: "My soul glorifies the Lord and my spirit rejoices in God my saviour…For he has done great things for me. Holy is his name" (Lk 1:46). She was the beneficiary of an amazing grace, which she could not have earned, she did not deserve, and no human acceptability could have induced. It was sheer grace from on high.[3]

Full of Grace

The angel greeted Mary with the words often translated as "Hail", but the Greek word used is more aptly rendered as "Rejoice!" Yes, she was to rejoice because God had chosen her for a unique place in the history of salvation. The greeting relates to the Old Testament prophecies where the same word is used: "Sing aloud, O daughter of Zion, rejoice and exult with all your heart, O daughter of Jerusalem" (Zeph 3:14); and again "Rejoice, heart and soul daughter of Zion! Shout with gladness daughter of Jerusalem! See now your king comes to you" (Zech 9:9). It's the joy of a heart opening to the wonderful in-breaking presence of God, not just personally but also amongst his people.

The Angel Gabriel continues by giving her the reason to rejoice. He calls her "highly favoured one". In an earlier era, this was translated as "full of grace". It is certainly about grace, but not only about grace already given, but also about the grace of the moment. She was being told that God looked upon her with great love. It is not so much about her already possessing all of God's gifts, but rather that she is being offered a new and powerful grace through God's favour and called to be receptive to this enormous gift. God's sovereign election was upon her. What had Mary done to merit being conceived holy and immaculate? What had she done to be preserved from original sin? What had she done to have the privilege of giving the Word his humanity? There is nothing. All is grace. Mary can certainly apply the words of Paul to herself, "By the grace of God, I am what I am" (1Cor 15:10). To say that Mary is full of grace sums up everything about her. Yes, she is the most beautiful human being, apart from Jesus, who ever lived, but this is all because of God's favour.

Chosen for Greatness

Through baptism, we all have been chosen by God. St Paul blesses God the Father and proclaims, "Before the world was made, he chose us, chose us in Christ, to be holy and spotless, and to live through love in his presence, determining that we should become his adopted sons, through Jesus Christ" (Eph 1:4-5). Mary knew herself this way in a quintessential manner. Chosen by God before she was conceived, she was elected for a key purpose in God's redemptive plan for the world. She received the grace to be a daughter of God in fullness even during this earthly journey. Now as daughter of Sion, she shares in the glorious resurrection of her Son. She is an inspiration for us on our pilgrim journey, and she assists us with her prayers as we seek to cooperate with God's grace and grow in holiness.

While it was all the result of grace, we know that Mary was predisposed towards the incarnation happening within her. God could pour out all of his gifts upon her because he found a humble and poor heart. She had lived a humble life with genuine poverty of spirit, open and available for God's coming. We remember the words of God, "With heaven my throne and earth my footstool, what house could you build me, what place could you make for my rest? All of this was made by my hand and all of this is mine, it is the Lord who speaks. But my eyes are drawn to the one of humbled and contrite spirit, who trembles at my word" (Is 66:1-2). This utter receptivity to God, which in itself is a cooperation with grace, drew the Lord to her. She knew that she did not deserve his glance, but in fact he had turned his countenance towards her with a love that knows no limit. He filled her with grace because he loved her. This love was totally gratuitous. But he found in her a free receptivity that allowed him to bring about the impossible in her.

The angel assured her, "The Lord is with you". These words no doubt were etched into her heart to sustain her in later times as she began to experience the agony of the role in salvation history, which was God's plan for her. More would be asked of her than any other person. She was to be the one to bear the incarnate Son of God for the world. The angel's word assured her of God's presence in the loneliness of that unique vocation. She will have the grace to endure whatever will come.

Mary's immediate reaction to Gabriel's greeting was consternation and confusion. She was shocked and couldn't offer a single word. This had all come out of the blue. Nothing had prepared her for this divine interruption in her daily life. The angel speaks to calm her, calling her by name for the first time, "Mary, do not be afraid, you have found favour with God". We are reminded of God speaking to Moses "as a man speaks to his friend" and says, "I know you by name and you have found favour in my sight" (Ex 33:12). Again, it is absolutely gratuitous favour, freely given and without strings attached. God "abounds in grace and faithfulness, keeping his favour for thousands" (Ex 34:6). Mary has received God's favour and election. She has been loved unconditionally and transformed by this love.

Under God's Mercy

This phrase of being under God's favour is closely related to the experience of God's mercy. The Lord said to Moses, "I will be gracious to whom I will be gracious, and I will show mercy on whom I will show mercy" (Ex 33:19). Grace and mercy abound where God is truly present and active. In her Magnificat Mary three times extols God for his mercy. She knew his mercy most deeply, not because she had sinned, but because she had been preserved from sin. She was full of gratitude because she knew the cavernous depths of human lostness from which the Father had rescued her by no merit of her own. Not having known the stain of sin, she still knew more than anyone the poverty of our human condition, from which grace alone has saved us. Paul expressed it well, "For by grace you have been saved through faith; and this is not our own doing, it is the gift of God" (Eph 2:8). We are only able to be who we are by the mercy of God. The Blessed Virgin is a supreme example of this.

Mary's place in the plan of God speaks powerfully of the absolute superiority of grace over nature, but it also speaks of how grace builds on nature and brings us to wholeness. It is grace that heals the human being from our deepest wounding and transforms us into the new creation of God. In the theology of grace, we tend to make a distinction between "uncreated grace" which is the indwelling presence of the Holy Spirit within us, and "created grace" which is the change that takes place in us due to this abiding presence of Christ within. This transformation brings about a life of virtue, which is what we call holiness. In Mary, we find both the fullness of God's favour through his abiding presence within her soul and also the fullness of personal holiness. She is God's masterpiece. She is the example of what can happen to a human being who welcomes the Holy Spirit completely.

Let Beauty shine

Since Mary is the mirror of the Church, we need to pray that something of her beauty would radiate in the life of the Church today. Her beauty was not skin-deep. It was the beauty of a soul untouched by sin. Even the greatest saints were sinners. They had flaws in their make-up. But Mary was radiantly beautiful in her poverty of spirit and her total orientation towards God. She was immersed in God's word and full of love for all. She was not like the glamorous celebrities of our day, who are so often glossy on the outside but with deeply ingrained personal struggles. She did not seek the limelight, but kept her heart wholly for God. May something of her beauty be found in the Church today! Beauty attracts souls, because it is a reflection of the beauty of God. We are the holy people of God, but unfortunately, there is much sinfulness in the Church. The only answer, guided by Mary, is deeper conversion under the grace of the Holy Spirit. How much these days we need the true joy of Christ to invigorate the Church and be evident in how we live together and relate within the world. Mary's presence can call us back to being centred in Jesus and more open to the changing work of the Spirit.

St Paul warns us as fellow workers of Christ, "not to accept the grace of God in vain" (2Cor 6:1). We must not presume on grace, nor should we neglect it. There is an urgency when we are moving under the anointing of the Spirit. The grace of God is within us. By "grace", we don't mean a thing we possess, or an idea we hold, but living contact with a person. Grace is simply "Christ in you, your hope of glory" (Col 1:27). Grace is the gift of the Holy Spirit within us so Christ dwells in our hearts by faith (cf. Eph 3:16). This gift needs to be kindled again and again. Paul urges us to "fan into a flame the gift given to you when hands were laid upon you" (2Tim 1:6). Having received grace upon grace we must not squander this immense gift, but respond wholeheartedly to God in faith, gratitude and wonder. With Mary, we must believe in grace: that God loves us unconditionally, that he pours out his Spirit upon us, and that his favour is upon us as his beloved sons and daughters. We must also be deeply grateful for the grace given to us so freely by God. We join with the whole Church daily singing Mary's Magnificat, "My soul glorifies the Lord, my spirit rejoices in God my Saviour". We praise God for his merciful love because he has looked upon his lowly servant. He has met us in our brokenness, lifted us from our poor, wretched condition, and given us new life in him. His amazing grace fills us with gratitude and our hearts exult with the Blessed Virgin. When we find ourselves needy and helpless, aware of our incapacity for virtue, and maybe assailed by a thorn in the flesh, we hear the Lord whispering as he did to Paul, "My grace is enough for you, my power is at its best in weakness" (2Cor 12:10).

2

COURAGEOUS FAITH

After her initial confusion before the angel, Mary had to ask the practical question. "How can this be? I do not know man", meaning that while she was betrothed to Joseph he had not yet taken her to his house. It was not yet time for them to come together and any sexual relationship was out of the question. She wanted to cooperate with God's plan, but how could this purpose be fulfilled?

Zechariah and Mary

To gain an insight into Mary's faith we can compare her response to that of Zechariah who had also been visited earlier by the same Gabriel (Lk 1:5-22). While Zechariah was attending to his priestly duty in the Holy of Holies, the angel appeared and announced to him that his wife Elizabeth would have a child. This was blatantly impossible since they were both getting on in years and, in any case, Elizabeth had been barren all their married life. Zechariah's response contrasts with that of Mary. Like most of us he wanted a sign, "How can I be sure of this?" He doubted the word of God. As a result the angel replies, "I am Gabriel who stand in God's presence, and I have been sent to speak to you and bring you this good news. Listen! Since you have not believed my words, which will come true at the appointed time, you will be silenced and have no power of speech until this has happened!" Such are the consequences for those who do not believe the word of God!

Mary, on the other hand, did not demand a sign, nor did she doubt the angel's word, she simply wanted clarification on an obvious problem that seemed insurmountable for God's word to actually happen. She knew by what the angel had announced that she was to be the mother of the long awaited Messiah. The description that her son would be a king of David's line and would rule over the house of Jacob with a reign that will last forever would have clearly revealed the angel was talking about the Messiah. Any devout young Jewish woman would have got the message. But how could this practically happen? Her question gave Gabriel the opening to make it clear. The Holy Spirit would come upon her and she would be overshadowed by the power of the Most High God. And to make it even more emphatic the angel continued, "And so the child will be holy and will be called Son of God". That would certainly have given Mary pause as she realised the immensity of what God was asking. And because, unlike Zechariah, she didn't ask for a sign, she was given one. Her cousin Elizabeth, the angel announced, who was in her old age and had never born a child was now in her sixth month of pregnancy. Then came the clincher, "for nothing is impossible to God". For the incarnation to occur all that needed to happen now was Mary's response.

Waiting for a Response

Bernard of Clairvaux has a marvellous meditation on this moment.[4] The angel has proclaimed God's word. He awaits a response. Bernard pictures Adam, Abraham, David and all the holy fathers waiting eagerly for her response – all hanging on her "yes" to the plan of God. This was the hinge of our salvation.

> Answer, O Virgin, answer the angel speedily; rather through the angel, answer your Lord. Speak the word, and receive the Word; offer what is yours, and conceive what is of God; give what is temporal, and embrace what is eternal. Why delay? Why tremble? Believe, speak, receive!

In Bernard's mind the whole of heaven and earth is waiting with bated breath for the answer of the virgin,

Open your lips to speak; open your bosom to your Maker. Behold! The Desired of all nations is outside, knocking at your door.

He urges her to rise up, run by the devotion of her heart, and open her lips to answer.

Mary said, I am the handmaid of the Lord; let it be done to me according to your word. (Lk 1:38)

Radical Faith

The wonderful reality was that Mary believed, and thus she became the "Mother of the Lord". Mary's response in those few words was the most decisive act of faith in all of history. She was passively willing to yield to the Lord's will, but she was also actively ready to do whatever was demanded. She totally emptied herself so that she could be filled to overflowing. In just a few words, which have echoed down through the centuries she offered herself to God as a clean page on which he could write whatever he desired. While she questioned the 'how' of God's plan she did not expect or demand to know the blueprint.

She sought an explanation to understand how it could happen but she did not seek a crystal ball for the future. Her future was now radically in the hands of the Lord. Her "yes" was not only for her future, but it was a yes for all humanity. Mary became the new Eve. While she was still a virgin the first Eve had accepted Satan's word, and lacking trust in God had fallen into disobedience. With her the whole of the human race fell. Now the virgin of Nazareth accepted the word of God, and putting her trust fully in God, made the act of obedience, which became the doorway for all humanity to be redeemed by the Saviour conceived in her womb. Created freedom had failed with the original Eve, but now with the new Eve human freedom was given a new chance for redemption.

Mary's True Greatness

The greatness of Mary is not merely in her being the one who conceived and carried the Christ-child in her womb, giving birth to the Son of God. As the Fathers used to say, "she conceived the Word first in her heart, and then because of this she conceived the Word in her womb"[5]. The primacy is with obedience to the word of God. And this is what makes her the first disciple. St Paul begins and ends his letter to the Romans by saying his whole purpose was to bring the Gentiles to "the obedience of faith" (Rom 1:5, 16:26). Faith is not complete without obedience. Even the demons believed Jesus was the Son of God, but they would not obey.

Genuine faith in God requires a commitment in relationship, which calls for a surrender of the whole person to the will of God. Mary is the prime example of this sort of faith. Faith is proven through the doing of God's word. Otherwise, it may simply be a good idea, or adherence to an ideology, and not really a whole-hearted commitment to God. When the woman in the crowd cried out to Jesus, "Blessed is the womb that bore you and the breasts you sucked" he replied immediately, "Even more blessed is the one who hears the word of God and keeps it" (Lk 11:27-28). He is underlining the greatness of the Virgin Mary, his mother – not firstly due to her being his mother, but rather because she obeyed the word of God.

The Faith of Abraham

Mary is the model of "Abrahamic faith". As a daughter of Abraham, she brings the faith of Abraham to its highest point. The first critical moment for Abraham to exercise faith was when the Lord called him to leave his country, his family and his father's house and go to "the land that I will show you" (Gen 12:1). There was no map, no watertight guarantees, but simply the promise of the Lord. He was to step out into the unknown trusting only in the word of the Lord that this journey would bring great blessings. Mary's trust in God is of the same quality. As Paul says, "Though it seemed Abraham's hope would not be fulfilled, he hoped and he believed" (Rom 4:18). Then when God had promised a child to Sarah, who was too old for childbearing Abraham's faith was not shaken. "Since God had promised it Abraham refused to deny it or even to doubt it, but drew strength from faith and gave glory to God, convinced that God had power to do what he promised" (Rom 4:20). This is the quality of Mary's faith also.

The second moment of faith for Abraham was when he "offered to sacrifice his only son even though he had been told: It is through Isaac that your name will be carried on" (Heb 11:17). Again, Abraham did not hesitate, nor did he try to calculate the cost involved or the consequences of what God was asking. He simply obeyed. Mary's response to the angel was the same. She stands at the end of a long line of faith-filled men and women of the Old Testament, now at a pivotal moment in the history of the world, and puts all her trust in God, not only agreeing to be the mother of the Messiah, but also surrendering all the unknown consequences of such an unconditional "yes" to God. Elizabeth's greeting of Mary highlights this Abrahamic faith, "Blessed is she who believed that the promises of the Lord would be fulfilled in her" (Lk 1:45).

3

BOUNDLESS TRUST

Mary's act of faith speaks of boundless trust in God. This issue of trust is fundamental to all who embark on the spiritual journey. The deepest struggle in the human heart is to truly trust the Lord. Where do I put my trust? Do I trust in God and surrender to his will? We would like to yield to the will of God but we find ourselves incapable of doing so. We may blame the pressure of our circumstances, or a depression of spirit, or weakness of will, or fear of the unknown. But these "reasons" amount to excuses. Even Mary was not beyond these temptations. She was free to refuse God's offer to her. She was faced with the same choice we face, expressed so clearly by Moses: "See, I set before you today blessing or curse: a blessing if you obey the Lord your God, a curse if you disobey" (Deut 11:26-27). Beatitude will come through faith and hope; disaster will come if you choose the other path.

Having a Humble Heart

In order to trust God we must be humble, looking not to ourselves and what reserves of wisdom or energy we have, but rather looking solely to God. This is why Jesus says, "Unless you change and become like little children you cannot enter the kingdom of God" (Mt 18:3). He does not mean being childish which is always self-centred, but being child-like in so far as a child is totally dependent on the parent. In the spiritual life, we may begin the journey with great generosity of heart, but if we put our trust ultimately in our own generosity, it will eventually fail us. It is not our own grit and tenaciousness that will see us through the trial of faith, but rather our total trust in God and dependence upon him.

The big temptation for the generous-hearted person is to press on stoically through any trial regardless of the cost and conditions; the fallacy of self-sufficiency, driven by a deeply ingrained pride. We don't want to let go of control of our lives. We want to remain in charge. So instead of turning to God alone, we fight through by ourselves. This is not the way of the Virgin Mary. Her life was one of continual supplication to God. She knew her utter poverty before the Most High God. She did not prefer her own judgement to that of God. She was simply supple in his hands. Jeremiah's prophesy applies to Mary: "A blessing on the one who puts trust in the Lord, with the Lord as one's hope" (Jer 17:5-7). That one is like a tree by the waterside, thrusting its roots into the stream. In the midst of drought, it never ceases to bear fruit. But he gives a warning, "A curse on those who put their trust in things of the flesh". They are like "dry scrub in the wastelands". Mary's choice was clear. She trusted in the Lord.

The spiritual journey can be imagined as a gradual ascent towards God. But, in fact, it is even more accurate to see it as a *descent* towards the awareness of our lowliness and incapacity, and the fundamental contingency of our being. It is a blessing to know intuitively the limitations of our broken human condition. From this place of neediness, we can only rely upon God and on nothing or nobody else. The Lord hears the cry of the poor; the crushed in spirit he saves. The humble and contrite heart he will not spurn. Therese of Lisieux reflecting on her life said, "abasing myself to the depth of my nothingness, I was raised so high that I was able to attain my end".[6] She loved the saying of John of the Cross, "I went down so low, so low, that I was finally able to climb up so high, so high, that I finally reached what I was longing for".[7] Mary rejoices in the mercy of God who looked upon her lowliness and preserved her from sin; we rejoice that he has also looked upon the lowliness of our fragile human state and made us into a new creation. "It was for no reason except his own mercy that he saved us, by means of the cleansing water of rebirth and by renewing us with the Holy Spirit" (Titus 3:5).

Knowing we are Loved

Fundamental to Mary's spiritual journey was her experience of God's love for her. She could do nothing else but rejoice in this love. Her great song of praise arises out of being overwhelmed by the goodness of God. She had been filled with the Holy Spirit, who is the love between the Father and Son for all eternity. As Paul says, "the love of God is poured into our hearts by the Holy Spirit" (Rom 5:5). She trusted fully in God's love for her. As John says, "We are the ones who have put our faith in God's love for us" (1Jn 4:16). This joy of being loved by God is deeper than any feeling. Prayer may sometimes be full of affection and inspiring revelations. But at other times, it can be as dry as chips or a monumental battle. The feeling level is not what is important. Mary shows us the meaning of prayer. It would be naive to think that Mary went about her day and through all of the moments of her life full of pleasant touches from God and rushes of emotional love for him. It is dangerous if our prayer becomes self-centred, seeking experiences rather than the Lord himself, wanting the gifts rather than the Giver. Mary did not fall into that trap. She was taken into the darkness of faith in which she knew God's love for her more deeply than during any uplifting emotion.

The knowledge of God's love was written into Mary's being; it was the prevailing state in which she lived at all times. Whether emotions were present or not was of little consequence. She "knew" God in the biblical sense; a knowing akin to the union of husband and wife in marriage. Mary's faith was a nuptial "yes" of a bride to her bridegroom. The prophet's words applied to her, "I will betroth you to me forever...I will betroth you to me in steadfast love" (Hos 2:13). She knew that God had taken her to himself, and given her the "kiss of love". She was pursued by the love of God and she freely allowed herself to be won by him. She could pray with all her heart, "I am yours", because she knew at the core of her heart the whisper of the Father, "You are mine". She knew his jealous love for her and this love urged her to give herself entirely to God. The depth of this commitment was not dependent on any rushes of emotion or fiery inspirations. It was a union of love, which was unbreakable because of the grace given and her unconditional response.

Overcoming Fear

Fear robs us of trust. We become paralysed and incapable of moving forward. No wonder the words "Do not be afraid" appear so often in Scripture. Someone once counted the number of times the command not to be afraid appears in the bible. They came up with 366 times; that is one for each day of the year, and an extra one just in case it is a leap year! When Mary was disturbed by the angel's greeting she was told, "Mary, do not be afraid". Notice she was addressed by name. This is not accidental. In Isaiah the Lord says, "Do not be afraid, for I have redeemed you; I have called you by name, you are mine" (Is 43:1). We remember Mary Magdalene weeping outside the tomb distressed because the body was missing. When she pleaded with the man she thought was the "gardener", he addressed her by name, "Mary!" (Jn 20:16). At that moment, the scales fell off her eyes. She knew him! When he calls by name, it is an invitation into intimacy and a revelation of his tender love for the one who he is addressing. He urges gently "do not be afraid". As our lives unfold over time again and again, like the Blessed Virgin, we need to hear those reassuring words whispered in the depth of the heart. The Lord says, "Do not be afraid, for I am with you; stop being anxious and watchful, for I am your God. I give you strength, I bring you help" (Is 41:10).

Fear is fed by negative thinking. FEAR stands for False Evidence Appearing Real. Our perception of the situation, and the ideas evoked by that, lead us into worst-case scenario thinking. We are governed by the "what ifs" and become paralysed from moving forward. Just as the sun breaks through a morning fog and visibility is restored, so the enlightenment of faith helps us see the truth through the fog in our minds. We have to deal with "stinking thinking"; combatting the lies within the mind with the truth of God's word. Jesus said, "If you make my word your home you will indeed be my disciples, you will learn the truth and the truth will set you free" (Jn 8:31-32). Mary lived by the word of God, not allowing the lies of the enemy to influence her.

In our life journey, God has a way of surprising us, just as he did with Mary. He likes to come to us in our poverty and weakness, choosing the most unlikely one for his purposes. Through his power at work in our weakness he saves, heals, and gives the strength we need for the vocation he gives us. All he asks of us is to trust him and to follow him. Mary did not hide her amazement that God had chosen her. She was no "high flyer". She was an unknown, ordinary young woman of Nazareth. She did not live in a mansion or have great wealth. She had not done any marvellous works that would draw the attention of her contemporaries. However, she was open to God, trusting in him. Pope Francis, meditating on Mary's challenge reminds us:

> God always surprises us, ruins our plans, makes a mess of our projects, and says to us: trust me, do not be afraid, let yourself be surprised, get out of yourself and follow me![8]

The challenge is not to become so beholden to a particular plan, a chosen profession, or a captivating ideology that we do not remain open to God disrupting our lives. Do I truly let God come into my life? How do I respond to him?

The journey of faith is always into the unknown, and never without trouble. Negativity can come against us and undermine us. The classic gospel story is that of Peter (Mt 14:22-33). The apostles were in the boat on the lake of Galilee, battling with heavy sea and rowing into a headwind. Jesus appeared out of the mist walking towards them across the water. They were terrified, thinking it might be a ghost. Jesus' words were "Courage! It is I! Do not be afraid!" Peter was bold enough to ask Jesus to give him the power to walk on water and come to the Master. Jesus simply said, "Come!" Faith involves a stepping out of the safety of the boat. It is just like walking on water; no longer progressing by your own power but by the help of the Lord.

Things were going well for Peter as long as he kept his eyes on the Lord. But it wasn't long before he realised how precarious his situation was. He felt the force of the wind and the waves. He lost sight of Jesus as he looked down at his feet, realizing this was impossible. Has anyone walked on water before? Peter begins to sink. This is what happens when negativity takes over in the midst of the storm raging around us. We lose focus on the Lord and collapse into introspection. But all is not lost. Peter knew from whom his help would come. As he is filled with dread at the prospect of drowning, he cries out to Jesus, "Lord! Save me!" Even when we have allowed negativity to swamp us, we can still call out to the Lord. His hand is never too short to save. Jesus put out his hand at once and lifted him up. What a beautiful description of the struggle for faith. Jesus chides Peter gently, "Man of little faith, why did you doubt?"

4

SURRENDER TO THE LORD

When Mary gave her initial "yes" to the Lord, she did this unconditionally. There were no "ifs" or "buts", no way of hedging her bets just in case things did not work out as hoped. Her whole life was on the line, given over to the unfolding plan of God for her. She completely surrendered herself into the hands of the Lord and in obedience to his will. In doing so, she had a very limited appreciation of what lay ahead of her and the degree to which her faith would be tested as life unfolded. In this way, she becomes a model disciple for us. When we first give our lives over to the Lord and say "I am yours", we cannot be expected to know what lies ahead. In fact, if we did have some preview of what was to come we may die of fright or at least be deterred from such a rash decision. In Mary's life, as in ours, there was a gradual unfolding of the fullness of the vocation which God had bestowed on her. Each step we take on this unknown journey, like Mary, we face a new set of circumstances. Our faith is challenged to make a deeper heart response to God. Let's look more closely at the faith journey of the Blessed Mother. This can give us inspiration and help in how to surrender to the Lord as each crisis occurs.

The Trial of Faith

The final sentence of Luke's annunciation story deserves much reflection. It says poignantly, "And the angel departed from her" (Lk 1:38). The great moment of Mary's encounter with the angel in which her whole life was changed now ends. No more angels are recorded as coming to her. She remains alone with the task before her that is beyond her human capacity, and with no human guide to help her. Totally reliant upon God she must take the path of a disciple, which inevitably will have many dark moments. She will often be left alone in the darkness of faith waiting upon the Lord to reveal the way to move forward, patiently learning what it means to be fully given to God.

From the very beginning, Mary suffered a trial of faith. She had to live with the shame of being pregnant out of wedlock. More than that, she knew that in her culture to be found with child when she had not yet come to Joseph's house was a crime worthy of death. Carlo Carretto[9] shares how while he was with the Tuaregs in the Sahara he discovered that a girl in the camp was betrothed to a boy in another camp. Because she was still too young, she hadn't yet gone to live with him. This reminded him of how Mary was betrothed to Joseph, but they had not yet come together. Two years later Carlo came back to the same camp and in casual conversation asked people whether the marriage had yet taken place. People greeted his question with embarrassment and awkward silence. But later in the day, he happened to meet one of the chief's servants at the village well. He asked the servant why people went silent on the topic. The servant looked cautiously around and then, because he trusted Carlo as a holy man, made a well-known sign amongst the Arabs. He passed his hand under his chin to indicate she had her throat cut. Before the wedding, it was revealed that she was pregnant. The honour of the betrayed family required that sacrifice.

Carlo realised for the first time the plight of Mary's loneliness when she fell pregnant. What could she say? "There was no father"? Who would believe this? How could she explain what had taken place in her? Who would believe her if she declared the child within her was the work of the Holy Spirit? She would have known that the law of Moses was exacting for a young woman if the signs of virginity were not found in her: she would be dragged to the door of her father's house and stoned to death by the men of the city (Deut 22:20f). It gives extra poignancy to her cousin Elizabeth's greeting, "Blessed are you who believed"!

Someone once said that faith is spelt "RISK". How true this is. And for Mary it was not an intellectual risk, but her life was on the line. She was thrown completely into the arms of Father God. She was the first to believe without seeing. Thankfully, God spoke to Joseph in a dream. Joseph had intended to quietly put Mary away out of danger. But he was told the child was conceived by the Holy Spirit and he was to take Mary into his care. Joseph is brought into the secret, "She will give birth to a son and you must name him Jesus, because he is the one who is to save his people from their sins" (Mt 1:21). What drama for this young woman! How she must have implored God for understanding in her distress and for strength to endure!

The Obedience of Faith

Hebrews tells us of Jesus: "During his life on earth, he offered up prayer and entreaty, aloud and in silent tears to the one who had the power to save him from death...Although he was Son he learnt obedience through suffering" (Heb 5:7-8). In the same way at each step of her pilgrim journey Mary implored God, aloud or in silent tears, for the strength to endure. In each crisis that came upon her, she was called to a deeper place of surrender to the Lord's will. She too learnt obedience through suffering. This does not mean that she was ever disobedient, but that there was a constant deepening of her "yes" to God. This was especially facilitated through the suffering the Lord allowed her to experience. As with Jesus, at these difficult times the prayer of supplication rose from her heart, imploring God for his help. She knew the poverty of our human existence without God, and humbly called upon him at all times. And as she continued on the journey with her Son, much suffering was to come. Each new calamity was an invitation to a deeper surrender of heart. The love in her for God could not increase, but each trial was an opportunity for a deeper release of this love, an enlarging of her heart in giving herself completely to God.

A Sword will Pierce Your Soul

When they brought the newly born Jesus to the Temple the encounter with Simeon left Mary in no doubt about the journey ahead. Simeon we are told was a righteous man, living according to the word of God. He is also described as a "devout" man, whose whole life was oriented towards God. And finally we are told he was a man "longing for the consolation of Israel". Getting on in years, he longed to see the salvation that would come with the expected Messiah. Taking the child in his arms, he delivered a prophecy in the Spirit. He declared he can now die peacefully because "my eyes have seen the salvation which you have prepared the nations to see, a light to enlighten the gentiles and the glory of your people Israel" (Lk 2:29-32). Mary's heart must have leapt at this confirmation of who her child really was. We are told Joseph and Mary stood in wonder at the words being said about their son.

But the joyful good news must come through the Cross. Simeon's prophecy now turns towards Mary. He foretells the passion, and its impact upon her. This child is "destined for the fall and rising of many in Israel". He will be a "sign that is rejected"; sobering words, which Mary must have pondered over often, especially in later years as she watched the inevitable collision course of her son with the religious authorities. But then Simeon's words were directed to Mary herself, "and a sword will pierce your own soul too". The journey would involve sharing in the agony of Jesus for the sake of the world. The full implications of this were yet to be revealed. We can be sure the words did not paralyse her with dread. But no doubt, she was shaken. It was a clear warning that the worst was yet to come. She would have experienced the normal human reaction to such a foreboding word.

However, Mary's grace-filled faith in God was such that she was ready to undertake whatever was asked of her for the love of God.

Terror of the Night

Almost immediately, the little family was thrown into crisis. Afraid of what the wise men had predicted, and realising they had tricked him, Herod planned to slaughter every male child under two years of age. Joseph was warned in a dream to flee as quickly as possible (Mt 2:13). The same night they fled to Egypt becoming refugees in a foreign country. Again, the Blessed Virgin experienced unexpected and chaotic displacement. We know from our present day experience of refugees this trauma can severely disrupt psychological stability and leave scars for life. The terror of the flight by night in order to protect their child must have called forth all their spiritual reserves as they once again trustingly placed their lives in the providential care of the loving God.

Some years later after Herod's death, they were able to return safely and settle in their hometown. Thus began the long period of the "hidden life" in the house at Nazareth. Mary lived this time as the one "who believed that the promises of the Lord would be fulfilled in her" (Lk 1:45). She lived with Jesus at her side, the son they had named "the one who saves" because of an angelic revelation to Joseph; the one who the angel had told Mary was "the Son of the Most High" (Lk 1:32). She knew he had been conceived in her without having relations with a man. All of this fed into her awareness of who Jesus was. However, Jesus later was to say, "No one knows the Son except the Father and those whom he chooses to reveal him" (Lk 10:22). Mary was the first chosen to have this revelation. She lived constantly each day in contact with the mystery of God in Jesus, her son. She knew by faith. She was the first of the "little ones" the Father chose to reveal the mystery. Yet this faith was not all light and splendour but shrouded in darkness as the incident when he was twelve years old indicates.

Returning from the festivities in Jerusalem with many relatives and others in a large caravan they each thought the child was with some other family members. But he had disappeared. Terror! Only parents who have lost a child or had one stolen can know fully what this fear is like. In those days, it was customary to traffic young boys to have them castrated and used as servants and protectors in harems. For three days, they searched frantically. Finally, they found him in the Temple with the teachers of the law. He was listening to them and engaging them in dialogue, showing a precociousness beyond his years. Joseph and Mary were obviously overwhelmed with relief when they saw him. This was disturbing behaviour. What did this mean? Mary asked, "My child, why have you done this to us? See how worried your father and I have been looking for you?" (Lk 2:48). His answer left them perplexed, "Why were you looking for me? Did you not know I must be about my Father's business?" His enigmatic reply was a presage of what was to come when he later launched out in ministry leaving his family bewildered. They did not understand. How could they? Yet we are told: "His mother stored up all these things in her heart" (Lk 2:51). Yes, she was confused and perplexed, but, as always, reflective, wondering what it all meant, yielding to the mysterious ways of God's unfolding plan.

Separation in the Public Ministry

When Jesus at the age of 30 years or so began his public ministry in Capernaum and other towns around Nazareth, word was filtering back to his relatives and other townsfolk that this previously sensible young man had gone crazy. Mark's gospel, which is the most primitive tells us that the crowds were gathering in large numbers and Jesus and his disciples were so busy they didn't even have time to eat. When

Jesus' relatives heard about this apparent madness "they set out to take charge of him, convinced he was out of his mind" (Mk 3:20-12). There is no mention of Mary in this text. We can surmise that she, who had a deeper insight into the meaning of her Son's journey, suffered greatly from being misunderstood in Nazareth also. The word around the town was that Jesus had gone bonkers, and again she had to endure this loss of face in silence and prayer. The gossip, mockery and maligning that she suffered was all part of the way of discipleship laid out for her.

This necessary distancing of Jesus from his mother during his ministry must have been truly painful for her. But in her reflections, she no doubt understood that it was part of the price paid for God's will to be done. An incident during the ministry of Jesus illustrates this. When "his mother and his brothers" arrived at a house where Jesus was teaching they could not go inside because of the crowd. They were forced to stand outside while they sent a message to Jesus conveyed through the crowd from mouth to mouth, "Your mother and your brothers are outside asking for you" (Mk 3:31-35). Did Jesus drop everything and run to his mother? No. She had already felt a premonition of this distance years ago in the Temple when he had been ministering to the doctors. However, she did not resent this necessary letting go. It was all part of her call to surrender to God's plan, within which she had a vital part to play.

She did not find his response offensive. It was simply the truth. Looking at his disciples in a circle around him he said, "Here are my mother and my brothers. Anyone who does the will of God, that person is my brother and sister and mother" (Mk 3:34-35). Jesus is once again spelling out the simple truth that the deepest relationship we can have with him is to share in his trust in the Father and obedience to his will. Mary is paramount example of this. Her greatness was not in her legitimate claim to be the one who carried him in her womb, gave birth to him in Bethlehem, and nurtured him in his infancy. All of that unique, unrepeatable privilege was immense. More important than this however, was her faith and obedience to God. There is her true greatness.

Sharing in the Passion

The inner pain of Mary deepens in intensity as Jesus' passion begins. While it is not recorded in the gospels, tradition gives us a beautiful image of Mary meeting Jesus as he carries his Cross to Calvary. Her presence in the passion of Jesus is not accidental. She is destined to be the image of the Church's holiness. All who are responding to the call to holiness will find the only way forward is through the Cross. "If anyone wants to be a follower of mine, let him renounce himself and take up his cross and follow me" (Mk 8:34). The meeting of Jesus with his mother on the way to Calvary is worth lingering on in prayer. Few words, if any, would have been spoken; yet a communication of one soul to the other, one heart to the other. The eyes meet with tenderness and mercy, a pool of consolation in the midst of unimaginable hatred, cruelty and brutality. It was a moment of mutual encouragement, bringing strength to one another; a determination to yield together to the Father's will for the sake of the world.

While Mary would not have been able to fully appreciate the significance of what was happening, she faithfully put her whole trust in God, and in her Son who with his eyes reassured her that this was the way the kingdom he preached would be realised. She surrendered in the darkness of Calvary. The "yes" she originally made in Nazareth 33 years previously had already been deepened and her heart enlarged in love through so many vicissitudes. Now was the final journey of discipleship; a new grace upon her to go the distance with Jesus unto the Cross.

Standing at the Foot of the Cross

Then we come to the crucifixion itself. How did this mother endure such agony? Watching her son being nailed to the wood of the Cross, his body wrenching in convulsions of pain, and hearing his words, "Father forgive them for they know not what they do" (Lk 23:34). She also finds the grace of forgiveness in her heart; she knows implicitly mercy is coming to the world now like never before. She accepts the grace that is being poured out through her Son's sacrifice. But she also shares with him in his offering to the Father. St Bernard tells us that the wounds that Jesus experienced in his hands and feet Mary experienced in her heart. Truly, Simeon's prophecy is fulfilled, "and a sword will pierce your own soul too". She stood there with John the Beloved and others offering her life with Jesus.

After he expired, she saw the sword pierce his heart from which flowed blood and water. "He was pierced through for our faults, crushed for our sins. On him lies a punishment that sets us free. By his wounds we are healed" (Is 53:5). As she is drawn into the mystery of the Cross Mary finds her heart enlarged even more in love. The love blazing in the heart of her crucified Son blazes in her heart also. As horrible as Roman crucifixion was, she was not crumpled into a heap of self-pity, full of uncontrollable grief and distress. She knew this is how it must be. This was the ultimate unfolding of the plan of salvation within which she had been asked to cooperate. Her love expands, her hope is sustained, yet her motherly agony is almost unbearable. She is consoled by the knowledge that all of this is within the mysterious purpose of God.

Self-emptying love

The normal path to sanctity takes us through purification and deprivation. After the initial grace of deeper conversion, our faith and love for the Lord is tested. Writing to the early Christians under persecution Peter reminds them of the "sure hope" they have in the resurrection of Christ (1Pet 1:3-9). Having encountered the risen Christ is a cause of great joy for them, even though they must bear many trials and tribulations. Their faith must be tested like gold in the furnace, purged of all impurities. This is a great privilege since it is the way to sanctity, union with God.

In our journey of discipleship, our faith must be purified. Our love for the Lord needs to be strengthened through suffering. After having experienced a new infilling of the Spirit and awakened in a new love for him it is more than likely that in time the Lord will remove our customary supports and we will be taken to a new level of dependence upon him. The darkness of faith arrives. Mary is our guide and model in how we should behave when this time of pruning begins. St John Paul II speaks of Mary as the model for self-emptying love.[10] The Greek word is "kenosis"; the classic text is given by Paul in describing Jesus' self-emptying: "Christ Jesus, though he was in the form of God, did not count his equality with God a thing to be grasped, but emptied himself" (Phil 2:6-7). This is the fundamental dynamic of any discipleship, and Mary is our best model.

Mary's pilgrimage of faith was not all lights and miracles. After the initial encounter with the angel she was soon plunged into the night of faith. St John Paul II speaks of Mary's intimacy with Jesus as precisely this darkness through which she was drawn more deeply into the mystery of the passion and Cross of Jesus. "Through faith Mary is perfectly united with Christ in his self-emptying". It began, he says at the Annunciation, and then continued through her whole pilgrimage of faith, reaching its climax at Calvary. He says, "At the foot of the Cross Mary shares through faith in the shocking mystery of this self-emptying. This is perhaps the deepest 'kenosis' of faith in human history."[11]

A Font of Grace

Standing at the foot of the Cross on Calvary Mary becomes an example for all who are faced with bewildering loss, or unexpected calamity, or debilitating suffering, whether physical, psychological, relational or spiritual. Suffering no longer can destroy us; Jesus has redeemed it. Mary can be our way into the experience of that redemption. As we have been following her path of discipleship, we have discovered that as each calamity occurs Mary digs deeper for a more large-hearted response. In each new time of testing her heart expands in love. She shows us how unexpected shattering experiences become an opportunity for a deeper "yes" to the will of God. Instead of being destructive, they become fonts of life for the believer.

St John Paul II wrote that in Christ, "God has confirmed his desire to act especially through suffering, which is man's weakness and emptying of self, and he wishes to make his power known precisely in this weakness and emptying of self"[12]. One of the most profound experiences of adult life is the loss of control, which comes through suffering. We are often reduced to being dependent on others and incapable of holding ourselves together. This loss of control can be awfully disorienting and the accompanying feelings severely debilitating. No matter what happens and how terrible it becomes, if through Mary we unite ourselves with the mystery of the Cross, we will find a font of life both for ourselves and for others. As St John Paul II remarks, "The springs of divine power gush forth precisely in the midst of human weakness".[13] In and through our sufferings, when we join with Mary in uniting them with the suffering of Jesus, we find a font of grace, and we can become a font of grace for others.

A Mother's Pierced Heart

The Blessed Virgin Mary is the ultimate model of being a disciple. Many parents experience with Mary the sword piercing their hearts as they grieve over the waywardness of their children. Judy was heart-broken as she helplessly watched her first-born son, Christian, sink ever more deeply into seemingly hopeless drug addiction.[14] How many mothers have suffered as they have helplessly watched their child succumb to this affliction? Judy had previously wandered from the Catholic faith into a friendly evangelical circle. But she was drawn back through hearing of Marian apparitions which made her wonder whether Mary could mend her broken family. Surprisingly she experienced a dream, which she knew was the presence of the Blessed Virgin promising to bring healing to her family.

Judy began to realise that Mary's secret was her utmost trust in God no matter what the circumstances. She realised that maybe it was God's plan for her heart to be pierced also. She began to see that, while life is messy, God is in the mess. This was the message of the manger in Bethlehem and also the revelation of the Cross. The stable at Bethlehem and the Cross reveal the paradox of the Christian journey of discipleship. When we are weak we become strong; when we are poor we become rich; and when we die to ourselves we find life.

Judy knew within her heart that nothing could compare with the love she felt for her child. The suffering of a child can pierce the heart of a mother, humble her to the core, and leave her devastated. No other experience on earth can match a mother's love. It is a unique glimpse of the tender, fierce love of God for each one of his children. Motherhood is filled with great joys, but being a mother can mean dying a thousand deaths. Judy began to welcome the presence of Mary since she knew what it was to suffer as a mother. Mary is particularly close to mothers. Her experience is theirs, and their experience is hers.

Christian's life was reeling out of control. Judy turned more and more to the Blessed Virgin Mary, who shows us how to stand firm in suffering without becoming hard of heart. Mary intercedes for us when we cry out to her. She is especially touched when a mother pleads for her child. This is a cry she knows Jesus cannot ignore. The tears of the widow of Nain for her only son as he was being carried out for burial touched the heart of Jesus. He did not hesitate, "Young man, rise up!" (Lk 7:15) Mary loves to bring the worst cases to her Son.

Yet it was a long journey for Judy. More than once, she thought she had lost her son forever. Multiple rehabilitation programs and interventions had not worked. They had tried everything. When his dad died early, Christian spun totally out of control. Judy had to resort to tough love and put Christian out of the home. It was the hardest thing she ever had to do. A mother's natural drive is to save her child; this seemed the opposite. But she knew that it was probably his last hope for survival. She had been advised that the shock of putting the boy on the street might force him to seek help. It didn't; at least not at first. He found others who would give him a bed and drug handlers who would continue his supply. All she had left was prayer.

Judy prayed constantly giving him over to Jesus and Mary. Her son's condition escalated provoking major interventions. But it was going nowhere. Judy kept praying for help. At a healing Mass Judy was challenged by the priest to surrender everything into the hands of the Lord. There was a new grace to do so. God had brought about a much-needed shift, not firstly in her son, but in Judy herself. Once she released her son into the Lord's hands, she found a new peace. All would be well. When Christian called again she was calm, poised and confident. She had stepped out of the grip of the addiction and now lived in the rare atmosphere of surrender to God. Two days later Christian rang again. He had contacted a community called Cenacolo to apply for orientation to join the community!

Judy knew this community. It was founded by Sister Elvira in Italy and had a house at the foot of the hill of apparitions at Medjugorje, where Our Lady began appearing in the 1980's to a group of children. Now there are over sixty houses in different parts of the world.

Many young men have been rehabilitated from drugs through a simple program of prayer and work. Until now, Christian had flatly refused to even go near the community which was located in Augusta Florida. After the three-day orientation program the community leaders decided to make an exception to their established rule and take Christian immediately. Usually they give a two-week cooling off time before entry. The leader looked at Christian and said, "But you're not going to make it back here alive in two weeks if we let you go home." By the grace of God and Mary's intercession Christian lasted the three-year program and a mother's prayers had been answered.

5

CONTEMPLATIVE OF HEART

Mary walked with a contemplative attitude of heart. She wants to teach us to walk in the same way. Contemplation is a loving, attentive gaze upon Jesus, and also knowing within the depths of the heart the Lord's loving gaze upon us. No one was ever more devoted to contemplating the face of Jesus than Mary, his mother. No one has ever known more deeply the loving presence of God upon her at all times.

While Jesus was still in the womb, Mary was sensing his presence with the eyes of the heart, picturing his features, sensitive to every move he made. She held him in her womb with love beyond all telling. Then in the stable in Bethlehem, as she wrapped him in swaddling clothes and laid him in the manger we can readily imagine her tender motherly gaze upon her new-born son, just like every mother who is filled with awe and joy at the miracle of her child. Later, when she was so relieved to finally find him safe in the Temple, she gazed upon him, perplexed and with a plaintive question, "Son, why have you done this to us?" Then at Cana in Galilee, when the newly married couple were embarrassed, she turned to her Son for help. Her penetrating gaze upon Jesus, with a mother's heart, knew implicitly her Son's deepest feelings and desires, and she was able to anticipate his showing his glory. Then at the foot of the Cross, her deep sorrow as she suffered with her Son, gazing upon him as his whole body was contorted with agony, feeling with him, helpless to change anything, surrendering to the will of God, in full communion with him as he gave up his spirit.

We can imagine also Mary's gaze of joy upon her gloriously risen Son when he appeared to her after his resurrection. Now her maternal solicitude was transformed into total awe and wonder, leading to worship and adoration. Then fifty days later when the Holy Spirit came upon her and the others gathered in the Upper Room, how wonderful was her loving gaze upon Jesus, risen and glorified, how magnificent was the fire within her praising and worshipping him as Lord!

The Rosary as Contemplation

As we grow with the heart of Mary, we find ourselves drawn by the Spirit into the mysteries of Jesus' early life, ministry, passion, death and resurrection. Mary's experience of gazing upon Jesus becomes our experience. She provides a pathway into the mysteries. Praying the Rosary is meant to be more than a mechanical repetition of well-known formulas. This wonderful way of vocal prayer can actually lead us into contemplation. With the heart of Mary, we journey with her through the mysteries of Jesus. She knows them all so intimately and she wants to draw us into heart to heart relationship with Jesus. She wants our hearts to open more fully to know him and love him more. In all prayer, as Teresa of Avila says, what matters is not that we think much but that we do whatever increases our love[15].

The Rosary, as St John Paul II taught, is a "compendium of the gospel".[16] As we meditate with Mary on each of the mysteries we find ourselves being formed more in the "perfect knowledge of God's mystery, of Christ, in whom are hidden all the treasures of wisdom and knowledge" (Col 2:2-3). The Rosary, prayed reflectively, leads us into the inner knowledge of Christ. The Pope explains:

> We might call it Mary's way. It is the way of the example of the Virgin of Nazareth, a woman of faith, of silence, of attentive listening. It is also the way of Marian devotion inspired by knowledge of the inseparable bond between Christ and his Blessed Mother: the mysteries of Christ are also in some sense the mysteries of his Mother, even when they do not involve her directly for she lives from him and through him.[17]

The Rosary, then, is a method of contemplation.[18] After imagining the particular mystery for each decade being prayed, listening in silence to its meaning, turning to the Our Father and being lifted up towards him, we then pray the 10 Hail Marys. The centre of gravity of each Hail Mary is the name of Jesus, which keeps us focussed on the mystery being contemplated. The name of Jesus is the only name by which we can be saved. Its repetition with Mary is powerful for the soul. Mary loves us to pray the Rosary since it is her way of taking us more deeply into the mystery of her Son, particularly into the mystery of his incarnation, birth, childhood, ministry, passion, death, resurrection, ascension and sending of the Holy Spirit at Pentecost.

She Treasured and Pondered in her Heart

Mary's contemplative attitude is particularly evident in her pondering over her Son at critical moments on the journey. When the shepherds arrived at the stable in Bethlehem and found the baby lying in the manger they repeated what the angel had told them about him: "Today in the town of David a saviour has been born to you: he is Christ the Lord" (Lk 2:11). And they revealed to Mary and Joseph the angel had said they would find "a baby wrapped in swaddling clothes and lying in a manger". We are told, "everyone who heard it was astonished at what the shepherds had to say" (Lk 2:18). But, "as for Mary, she treasured these things and pondered them in her heart" (Lk 2:19). In the quiet and solitude of the house in Nazareth, she must have remembered all of this and held it closely in her heart, pondering its significance and surrendering to the mystery of God's plan unfolding in her life.

Again, when in the Temple after questioning her son about his behaviour, she receives the enigmatic reply, "Did you not know I must be about my father's business?" His answer could not have immediately satisfied her. She echoes the cry of many mothers bewildered by their child's behaviour, leading her to brood over him, wondering where this journey was taking them. We are told that after this incident he went with them to Nazareth and continued in obedience. The gospels relate no more significant diversions that upset the family as he was growing into adulthood. However, of Mary we are told, "she stored all these things in her heart" (Lk 2:52). The true contemplative is always pondering over the meaning of life's events and how God is at work in them. What is the Lord about? The contemplative is eager to do God's will and discovers hidden meanings in even the most perplexing situations. God is at work and will always bring good out of even the worst calamity.

This was Mary's contemplative attitude. She kept all these things in her heart. We can see from these two instances recorded that this was her perennial way. Her life, like ours was full of joys and sorrows; the joy of Jesus' birth, the amazing words of the shepherds, the love of Joseph, the peace of her family, the consolation of watching her son grow in "wisdom, age and grace". But there was also sorrow; the uncertain future, lack of shelter because there was "no room in the inn", the rejection and desolation to come, the reaction of relatives to her son's mission, and ultimately the Cross. Light and shadow, dreams and anxieties, all these things rose in her heart. She did not ignore these experiences of life. She reflected upon them. She went over them with God in her heart. She did not repress her sorrows, nor treat her joys with frivolity. She brought everything to God. She did not close herself off from life and its many ups and downs. She did not allow herself to be overcome by fear or suspicion or discouragement. She pondered the things that happened; holding them in her heart and inviting God to be with her as she tried to make sense of it all. She brought everything that happened whether it was good or bad, joyful or sorrowful, into dialogue with God. She shows us how to love God in and through everything and to give ourselves to others without reserve.

Dwelling on the Word

The secret of Mary is that she spent her life with the word of God. Prior to the visit from the Angel Gabriel, she had spent hours with the word daily. In many paintings Mary is depicted sitting in front of the angel at the Annunciation with the Scriptures in her hands. She was accustomed to listening to God and spending time with him. Because she was so open to the word of God, she was able to conceive the Word of God in her womb. The word was already her secret before the Incarnation. He was close to her heart. Then he took flesh in her womb. Mary's life was especially beautiful because her heart was set upon God, and she loved to dwell on his word daily.

Mary was not some glamour queen. She came from an ordinary family, living a humble life in Nazareth, a town not known as famous. Philip's question shows how it was commonly viewed as a backwater, "Can anything good come out of Nazareth?" (Jn 1:46) She did not live a life of wealth and ease, but faced many anxieties and problems. Until the Annunciation, she was a normal young woman from a tiny village that had no prominence in worldly affairs. She was brought up in the Jewish faith, open to getting married and having a family. We can be sure she loved the Scriptures.

The word of God was her daily food. Her family would have taught her to learn passages by heart. Even after the Annunciation, when Jesus was conceived, she remains a normal woman to all who knew her. It is not as if she lived in some mystical cloud out of touch with daily realities. She would have gone to draw water from the village well like the other women, worked hard as the wife of Joseph, shopped in the market and loved her family. Yet she was deeply contemplative, with her heart set upon the Lord at all times, listening to his word and seeking to do his will.

Silence and Solitude

We need to have silence and solitude for the grace of contemplation to grow. Mary's time in Nazareth, while caring for Jesus, participating in household chores and village activities, would have given her ample time for quiet with the Lord. As a model of discipleship she kept God at the centre of her life at all times, and allowed this attitude to be purified by time aside in silent adoration. We go to solitude to allow the Lord to lure our hearts to himself. The Spirit draws us into the wilderness to speak to the heart (Hos 2:16). In the quiet, alone with the Lord, we are able to shed any false self, which has been formed by the world. We discover more deeply our real self in God. Mary, who was "full of grace", moved in contemplative prayer to remain real before God and not take on the superficiality and falsity of worldly ways. The Holy Spirit helps us to live in the truth, rather than in self-deceit and illusion.

In silence and solitude, we discover our weakness and nothingness before God. Mary, the poor one of God, loved to be alone with God, affirming in her the experience of her lowliness, her nothingness, her utter poverty before God. But contemplation is not only a self-emptying; it is also being filled with the immense love of God, and his power to deliver us from evil, or anything that would hold us back from him. We discover his passionate desire for union with us. The gift of contemplation is yielding to this passionate embrace of the Lord, letting him take hold of us, letting him possess us.

Growing in the Heart of Mary

Mary's holiness is radiantly beautiful. She is totally pure of heart. We entrust ourselves to her "Immaculate heart". Jesus proclaimed, "Blessed are the pure of heart, they shall see God!" (Mt 5:8) This is our aspiration, but to bring it about by our own efforts is beyond us. The many desires in our hearts are often in conflict with God's purpose for us. How can we gain an "undivided heart"? How can the idols of our lives be shattered so we live only for God's kingdom and his righteousness? (cf.Mt6:33) The single-mindedness of the saints seems to elude us. This is when we can turn to our Blessed Mother. Holiness is a gift, for only God is holy. To the degree that his holiness dwells within us as a transforming influence, we become holy. This is the work of the Holy Spirit, changing our hearts, recreating us, and making us shine with the light of Christ. Mary is the one human being, apart from her Son, who is so fully animated with the holiness of God. We can turn to her, confident of her presence and help. She has allowed herself to be totally emptied of selfish desires and prideful thoughts. She is radiant with the love of God. We can ask her daily to keep us in her purity of heart.

The more we entrust ourselves to the Immaculate heart of Mary the more she can fashion our hearts in the attitudes of Jesus. She is perfection itself. Welcoming her presence, and giving our hearts to her, allows her to shape us in the way of Jesus. We rely upon the Holy Spirit to work deeply within us and sanctify us. As we cooperate with this grace, we grow in habitual attitudes and behaviours that we call virtues. We want to grow in faith, trust, and surrender of heart. We also want to grow in practical love, humility, generosity, and courage in witness. Because Mary is so full of grace, redolent with the Holy Spirit, she draws us more quickly into holiness. She is so filled with God's love that his holiness is found perfectly within her. As we entrust our hearts to her we find the Holy Spirit moves more speedily and effectively in bringing the transformation we need.

Eileen O'Connor: Mary Purity of Heart

Eileen O'Connor, who recently was recognised as a "servant of God",[19] suffered with spinal tuberculosis and severe spinal curvature. Called to serve the poor in the slums of Sydney she could not emphasise enough the need to yield one's life to the Immaculate Heart of Mary. Eileen, who spent most of her short life in excruciating suffering, was privileged with a deep mystical intimacy with the Blessed Virgin Mary. She experienced Mary as totally pure without any spot or wrinkle, sinless and without blemish, radiantly beautiful because she is totally suffused with the Holy Spirit. She encouraged her sisters of Our Lady's Nurses for the Poor to seek this purity above all else. The way to purification is through the crucible of suffering, and the self-denial necessary to overcome the unruly passions. Mary's purity is due to the holiness of God who created her that way.

Eileen wanted her sisters to seek God's purity and perfection. As Jesus said, "Become perfect as your heavenly Father is perfect". Eileen understood that the more we become pure of heart the more free we are to give ourselves to others in love.[20] Mary is the perfect example of this, and the more we draw close to her the more we can become capable of this purity of heart and capacity to love all whom we meet. Mary's purity of heart is not just another quality she had. It is her identity.

Eileen's little community of sisters in Coogee, who in 1915 were undergoing set-backs and difficulties in their foundation, were blessed by an unexpected appearance of the Blessed Virgin Mary. They were gathered together in Eileen's room. Eileen was comforting them and reminding them that the suffering they were experiencing was a share in the suffering of Jesus. In the room, there was a statue of Our Lady of the Immaculate Conception. A single candle lit the room. Eileen drew their attention to the statue. As they turned towards it, they saw the eyes open and close before them. The statue appeared about three times larger than usual. This was seen in the flickering light of the candle, which was dying.[21]

When the candle went out and the room was in darkness, a light appeared on the altar above Our Lady's statue. Eileen cried, "She is coming! She is coming!" The form of Our Lady grew more distinct with each moment. They could see plainly the crown on her head with a beautiful light. The women were crying out, 'Sweet Lady, let us see you more plainly". In response to their pleas, the vision turned and so the Nurses could see her. They were on their knees trying to pray, but that was not possible, so overwhelmed were they by what they were seeing. At the time, the group decided to keep the whole experience a secret since they were already under suspicion and suffering persecution. They did not want to provide any more ammunition for their detractors.

Teresa of Calcutta: Mary's Heart for the Poor

St Mother Teresa of Calcutta also had a great love for the Immaculate Heart of Mary and encouraged her sisters to "beg Our Lady to keep us in her Most Pure Heart so that we may love Jesus with an undivided love, an immaculate love like hers".[22] Mother Teresa understood that the Immaculate Heart of Mary was a heart of pure love. She saw in Mary's heart the virtues that she held dear and wanted her sisters to acquire – poverty of spirit, humility, silence, thoughtfulness, and haste in service.[23] While she considered all the Marian feasts important, the feast of the immaculate heart of Mary was the key. A strong interior life is most crucial for spiritual growth. Our actions flow from what is in the heart. If the heart is good then the fruits will be good. Mother Teresa wanted her sisters to be formed in the heart of Mary. All else would flow from this:

> In the heart of Our Lady Mother Teresa found a path and portal into the mystery of Jesus' love for us. The heart of Our Lady represented for her mankind's maximum response to God, our highest and fullest response to his thirst to love and be loved.[24]

Mother Teresa experienced the heart of Mary as fully united with Jesus in his self-emptying love. Therefore, her heart is most open to sheltering the poorest of the poor. The first home for the dying, which Mother Teresa established in Calcutta was on the grounds of the Kali Temple dedicated to Hinduism's goddess of death and destruction. She called the place *"Nirmal Hridoy"*, "Place of the Pure Heart"[25]. In this home of peaceful rest thousands of abandoned people on Calcutta streets who faced the lonely prospect of dying on the streets, found a place of warmth and comfort. Those who were alone and unloved could now "die like angels, loved and cared for". For Mother Teresa this home was the mystery of Our Lady's heart. For Mary is God's own *Nirmal Hridoy*, his own Place of a Pure Heart. She offers shelter to the poor and abandoned. She is refuge for all who suffer turmoil, rejection, abuse, hatred and destitution. In Mary's heart do we find hope, because it is a heart of mercy and tender love.

PART II

MARY AS OUR MOTHER

6

WOMAN, BEHOLD YOUR SON!

John's gospel provides us with a wonderful way of understanding Mary's role in our lives. She is our mother. We turn to the scene on Calvary: "Near the cross of Jesus stood his mother" (Jn 19:25). While Mary, the wife of Clopas, and Mary of Magdala were also there, the focus of Jesus was upon his mother and "the disciple he loved standing near her". This "beloved disciple" was John, the author of the gospel. Jesus speaks first to his mother, "Woman, this is your son". Then to John, "This is your mother". We are told "from that moment the disciple made a place for her in his home". What do we make of this?

At a normal human level, Jesus is providing for his mother in a caring way. Just as Joseph was deputed to look after Mary in her loneliness at the incarnation, now Jesus was assigning John to care for her when he was gone. In both cases, Mary was being uprooted by God's plan in her life. She was submissive to the way he was caring for her in her poverty. But there was much more happening than caring for Mary's future practical needs. Remember that John had run away with the other disciples when Jesus was arrested in the garden (Mt 26:31). He had been with Peter warming himself by the fire when Jesus was brought before Caiaphas.

Confronted with unexpected crisis, John went to water. His inherent weakness became evident. No doubt, he had found Mary in the crowd as Jesus was labouring under the heavy Cross on the way to Calvary. Mary's love, strength and faithfulness in this supreme moment of testing would have given him the courage to stand at the foot of the Cross rather than hide in the crowd like the other disciples. He was there on behalf of all of us who crumble in the midst of crisis. He was graced to be the sole evangelist who tells us how the side of Jesus was opened by a lance. Mary brought John to faithfulness. As a result, he became the witness of the heart of Jesus broken open in love for the world. She wants to do that for all of us. Mary's intimacy with Jesus crucified means she desires to bring all of us into this experience of Jesus' love, especially in our worst moments. If we trust Mary as our Mother, we can go to Calvary with her and find the strength to take up our cross every day as genuine disciples. When the darkness of the Cross comes upon us, she gives us the courage to stand with her and gaze upon the love of Jesus poured out for us from his pierced heart. This is our source of hope and freedom.

Woman

We need to notice that from the Cross Jesus addressed his mother as "woman". That reminds us of the scene at Cana in Galilee, when Mary had declared to Jesus, "They have no wine!" She was giving him a nudge to do something about it. His answer was "Woman, my hour has not yet come!" (Jn 2:4) At both Cana and the Cross Jesus is not just referring to her as his biological mother. Addressing Mary as "woman" had symbolic power. We saw earlier how in the latter part of the first century links were being made between Mary, mother of Jesus, and Eve the mother of all humanity. Mary was seen as the woman doing battle with Satan (Gen 3:15). She is identified as "the woman" who will crush the head of serpent. In Revelations, this is taken up as the "woman clothed with the sun…who brought a male child into the world, the son who was to rule all the nations" (Rev 12:1, 5). Mary is the new Eve, representing all of humanity made new through the victory of Christ.

At the Last Supper in John's gospel Jesus uses the image of a "woman" in childbirth to describe the sadness of his death changing through rebirth into the unmistakable joy of resurrection: "A woman in childbirth suffers, because her hour has come; but when she has given birth to the child she forgets the suffering in her joy that a man has been born into the world"[26] (Jn 16:20-22). This is an allusion to Mary, and indeed to all disciples. She must endure an anguish akin to the labour pains of childbirth, initiated at Cana, prolonged through his passion, and completed through the agony of his "hour" of glorification on the Cross. She first takes the path of all disciples who must pass through the suffering of the Cross to attain the joy, which Jesus ultimately brings to the world. She gives us the encouragement and fortitude to embrace the experience of the Cross, not as a path to despair, but as a way towards life and hope.

The Hour

The reference to Jesus' "hour" in John's gospel is highly significant. It refers to his "hour" of glorification, being "lifted up" on the Cross and "lifted up" in resurrection (Jn 3:14; 8:28; 12:32). It was his hour of kingly glory. On the Cross, which was his throne of love, his "hour" is being fulfilled. Through Pilate's unwitting instrumentality the words on the Cross declare he is "Jesus of Nazareth, King of the Jews" (Jn 19:19). He now rules forever. His garment was retained as seamless, a symbol of the unity of his kingship amongst his followers. His new family is being founded right at the foot of the Cross. His mother was crucial to this family. John the beloved disciple represented all those who are genuine disciples gathered with Mary, the perfect disciple. He was the one who rested on the breast of Jesus at the Last Supper in the upper room and he was first to reach the empty tomb, outrunning Peter. We are told, "he saw and he believed" (Jn 20:8).

The Gathering

At this moment with Jesus' mother and John the Beloved at the foot of the Cross the Church was founded. His mother and John represent all the children of God, drawn together by the Son of Man "lifted up" from the earth. Jesus had said, "when I am lifted up from the earth I will draw all to myself" (Jn 12:32). The evangelist wants us to see the gathering of all those who were in some way dispersed by the power of sin and Satan. It happens through the crucified and exalted Jesus. This is the high point of the gospel proclamation. Jesus is the one who brings unity through the laying down of his life for the sheep (Jn 10:17-18). Caiaphas had unwittingly made a profound prophecy when he announced that Jesus must die for the nation. John explains further: "and not for the nation only, but to gather into one the children of God who are scattered abroad" (Jn 11:52). This was the purpose of the death of Jesus.

The Cross became the place where the gathering of the children of God would take place. At that "hour" the church was born. His mother and the beloved disciple, together with others at the foot of the Cross represent this gathering.[27] The evangelist underlines this theme when he concludes with the words: "And from that *hour* the disciple took her to his home" (Jn 19:27). This is a new relationship. The mother of Jesus has become the mother of the disciple, John. However, more so, she has become the mother of *all* disciples. This is a command of Jesus. When he says to Mary, "Woman, behold your son" and to John, "Behold your mother" the language is prophetic. The prophets in the Old Testament used this language when they spoke authoritatively in the name of the Lord. It was a new decisive revelation of God's will for a new relationship between his mother and his disciple John, and hence a new relationship between his mother and all believers. This is why we can appropriately call her "Mother of the Church".

Taking Mary Into our Home

Having looked at the scriptural message it is now time to talk about its implications for our lived experience. Jesus gave his mother to us and instructed us to take her into our home. We are invited to make a home for her in our hearts. It is not just a matter of subscribing intellectually to contemporary exegesis and the teaching of the Church. How does this reality impact our lives? It is an invitation to a warm, affectionate relationship similar to what Jesus experienced in his earthly journey. It is having a heart of welcome and hospitality for her presence and her maternal influence in our lives.

We allow her to nurture us in the faith, teach us to pray, show us the way of Jesus, and guide us in his Spirit. We ask her to draw us into the heart of Jesus her Son, which she knows so perfectly well. We want her to take us more deeply into the mystery of the Cross which she endured so uniquely, helping us to discover the height, the length, the width and the depth of his love for us and for the whole world. We open ourselves through Mary to discover more deeply the mystery of Pentecost, the action of the Holy Spirit in our lives, and how we can, like her, respond to the call to holiness and evangelisation, which flows from this mystery.

It is particularly helpful to ponder the words of Jesus to the beloved disciple, "Behold your mother". He gave us to her so we can come under her maternal care and protection. This means we can confidently place ourselves under her loving, nurturing attention, in the same way that Jesus did during his days in Nazareth. She can form us as disciples. We can call upon her in times of need and in the hour of temptation, or when life goes pear-shaped and we find ourselves confused, anxious or depressed. She is a loving mother who speaks to our hearts words of encouragement and through her prayers covers us with her mantle of protection.

Our Teacher of the Ways of God

Maybe the title of Mary as "seat of wisdom" can help us here. In the Old Testament, wisdom is highly sought after: "Therefore I determine to take her to live with me, knowing that she would give me good counsel and encouragement in cares and grief...She knows what is pleasing in your sight and what is right according to your commandments" (Wis 8:9; 9:9). To take Mary to our home is something like this. Because she is fully in the Spirit, she is the source of all wisdom. We can take her as our companion and counsellor. She knows better than we do what God wants for us. If we learn to consult with Mary and listen to her in all of the experiences of life, she will be an indispensable teacher of the ways of God, guiding us in the ways of the Spirit. She has been given to us by Jesus as our teacher in the life of faith and discipleship. She has a plan for our lives, which is simply God's dream for each of us. She has God-given responsibility for nurturing us in the ways of the Spirit. We turn to her just as trusting children turn to their mother to know what is best to do.

Mary's presence can be more than just an occasional boost to our spiritual life. She can become for us a trusted mother who really cares for what is best for us, forming our hearts and protecting us from the evil one. As our brother, Jesus wanted to give us his mother to look after us. Just as she cared for Jesus as he was growing to maturity she cares for each of her own; all those who are baptised as sons and daughters in the Son through the Spirit. Her heart beats with the heart of God, a heart that is for all without distinction. She is the human face of God's infinite tenderness and mercy. We can confidently bring to her our deepest problems and entrust them to her. Just as she pointed the servants towards Jesus at Cana, she does so for us when our lives are lacking what they need. Mary gives us hope as she accompanies us in our strife, and shows us the goodness of God, restoring our courage, and leading us to the loving heart of God.

Mother of Tenderness

Mary as our mother protects us from being spiritual orphans.[28] When a person feels lost without a mother, lacking the tenderness of God, the heart is truly sick. If the heart is only looking after itself and its own interests, forgetting that life is a gift, the person becomes self-absorbed and a modern day orphan. In this narcissistic culture, we can forget we belong to others and share a common home. We become beholden to no one but ourselves. We lose our own dignity and no longer appreciate the dignity of others. We belong to no one and they do not belong to us. In the heart there is a huge loneliness and emptiness, and the heart grows cold and hard, lacking in mercy and compassion. How much we need to rediscover the tenderness in the heart of God, which Mother Mary brings to us! She brings us into the heart of God and into the warmth and tenderness of relationship with one another. We are no longer seeing human beings as objects meant to consume and be consumed, but as children of God, as family, as the people of God. We need to welcome her into our homes, into our families, into our communities.

Pope Francis encourages us to look into the motherly eyes of Mary.[29] We see her gaze upon us, which sets us free from orphanhood; a gaze that reminds us we are brothers and sisters; that we belong to one another. "We must learn to take care of life in the same way and with the same tenderness with which she took care of it; sowing hope, sowing the sense of belonging, sowing fellowship".[30] Through her womb, Mary learnt to listen to the heartbeat of her Son. She learned to be a mother. Jesus in his humanity was the first to receive the maternal tenderness of his mother. With her, he discovered his identity as Son. With her, he learnt to listen to the anguish, the joys and the hopes of the people who longed for the Messiah. With her, we also become more who we are meant to be.

Mary gives us the warmth of a mother, embracing us in our

difficulties. The revolution of tenderness, which her Son begun is found most poignantly in her heart. She exudes warmth and affection, kindness and goodness, mercy and compassion. She shows us that humility and tenderness are not signs of weakness, but of great strength. In the gospels, she does not make great speeches or insist on rights or privileges. She does not draw attention to herself or try to make her presence felt. She teaches us there is another way to live, the way of tenderness. We are not orphans. We have a mother. As Pope Francis says,

> Mothers are the most powerful antidote against our individualistic tendencies, against our isolation and indifference. A society without mothers would be not only a cold society but a society that has lost its heart, and has lost the "family feel". A society without mothers would be a society without pity, one that has left room only for calculation and speculation. Because mothers even at the worst of times, know how to bear witness to tenderness, unconditional dedication, the power of hope.[31]

The Pope recalls mothers who have for years daily visited their sons and daughters in prison, or laid up in a hospital bed.[32] He remembers those mothers who have stuck with their children enslaved to drugs, and have not stopped fighting to give their children the best. We have all seen on our screens mothers in refugee camps bearing with unspeakable suffering for their children; some who give their lives so that none would be lost. The Blessed Mother is such with her children. She has the mother's heart for each one of us, and this is the most humanising influence we can ever have.

When we look to our mother, we are freed to focus on what is really important in life. Through her gaze upon us and her loving presence with us, we can leave aside all the useless rubbish that has accumulated in our lives and discover again what really matters.[33] The Church is mother and fundamentally feminine. Mary, as mother of us all, is a beautiful gift to the Church for us to discover our true identity. It is characteristic of the masculine to abstract, define and impose ideas. However, the mother brings the feminine genius. She knows how to connect in the heart and to give life. We need our mother to help us from having an overly intellectualised faith, arguing about ideas and doctrines, and not able to know the tenderness of God and listen to others with attentiveness.

As we allow ourselves to be gazed upon by our loving mother, we can lift our eyes to her in our desperate need. The eyes are the window to the soul. As we gaze upon Mary's eyes, we see a reflection of heaven, an invitation into the peace of God. In her eyes we encounter the beauty of God and cannot help but be attracted. We are drawn away from the sinfulness in our life, which diminishes us as persons. She does not look upon us as "sinners" or "reprobates" or whatever negative view we may have of ourselves. She looks upon us with the merciful heart of God. She is refuge of sinners. She prays for "those who do not yet know the love of God"[34]. She beckons us to come, wounded as we are into her non-judgemental embrace, to find comfort and strength to turn from our sin and find new life in God. Her eyes bring light to every dark corner of the soul, not to condemn us, but rather to help us face our helplessness and throw ourselves every more fully upon the boundless mercy of God. She says, "Don't be afraid, my children, I am here, your Mother is with you. I will not abandon you".

Mary, Untier of Knots

Pope Francis has a particular devotion to "Our Lady Untier of Knots".[35] The image comes from St Irenaeus, and was used at Vatican II. As quoted earlier, Irenaeus said, "The knot of Eve's disobedience was untied by Mary's obedience; what the virgin Eve bound through her unbelief, the Virgin Mary loosened by her faith".[36]

While its original meaning was referring to original sin, the image is appropriate when we talk about our personal sins. Most of us have knots in our life, which we feel helpless to undo. Some of us have multiple knots, which cause us to be quite tangled inside. It may be an addictive pattern, or an incapacity to forgive, or a deep-seated anxiety, or an uncontrollably sharp tongue, or another of the many possible bondages with which we suffer. We come to our mother, like a child comes after suffering a hurt, crying for help. She has a way of getting our focus off the problem and onto the Lord. We allow ourselves to be embraced in love and taken by the hand. We find new courage to face the battle. She convinces us to have faith in the Lord and draw from the victory he has won over sin and the power of Satan. As we lift our eyes to her, we find the knot slowly becomes untangled. There is no radical surgery, but rather the accepting love of a mother, who affirms us in our worth as children of God and reassures us of the redeeming grace of God available to us. Her gaze instils in us a new faith and trust in God and we gain new confidence to rise up from our stupor and become the new creation we are meant to be. As our mother, she gave birth to the Lord, and now she presents us, reborn to the Lord.

Pope Francis declares that the future of the Church and the world will be impoverished without the gaze of Mary our Mother. One of the dangers for the world today is that we seek to go ahead without tenderness of heart. With Mary, we will be more likely to care for one another as persons, and be aware that we are all brothers and sisters, one family.

> A world that looks to the future without a mother's gaze is short-sighted. It may well increase its profits, but it will no longer see others as children. It will make money, but not for everyone. We will all dwell in the same house, but not as brothers and sisters. The human family is built upon mothers. A world in which

maternal tenderness is dismissed as mere sentiment may be rich materially, but poor where the future is concerned. Mother of God, teach us to see life as you do. Turn your gaze upon us, upon our misery, our poverty. *Turn to us thine eyes of mercy.*[37]

Our Mother who Protects Us

As our loving mother, Mary protects us in all our times of trial. We can invoke her help at any time. In the early days of settlement in Western Australia, Benedictine monks from Italy, under the leadership of Abbot Salvado, established a mission at New Norcia, 130 kilometres north of Perth. The monks worked hard to plant and produce crops. As Salvado recalled, "Father Serra directed the bullocks, while I guided the plough. Indeed, I can say I have watered the Australian soil with the sweat of my brow and with the blood of my lacerated feet". In 1847, they were able to build a chapel dedicated to the Most Holy Trinity. Salvado set up above the altar the treasured image of Our Lady of Good Counsel, given to them by Fr Vincent Pallotti, who was later canonised. Then in 1848 a bush fire, driven by strong winds, spread through the grass and was heading towards the sheaves of corn. The whole Mission was under threat. All hands fought furiously to stop the scorching blaze. But it was a losing battle. The situation seemed helpless. The monks were inspired to take the precious image of Our Lady from the chapel and hold it high over the corn against the on-coming fire. This act of faith in the power of Our Lady's intercession saved them. Immediately the wind changed and began to blow in the opposite direction. The fire died out. The Mission was delivered from danger. Salvado wrote, "Thus did we witness the protection granted by our Holy Mother". He reported that the aboriginal people had been astonished at the influence of the Blessed Mother and a large crowd gathered for the celebration of a Mass of Thanksgiving for their deliverance.

7

MOTHER OF THE CHURCH

This title for Mary was favoured by Pope Paul VI as the clear affirmation of Vatican II teaching that Mary is "figure of the Church". He taught that the Church as mother gives birth to sons and daughters through the action of the Spirit in the sacraments. Mary our Mother "cooperates in their birth and development with a maternal love."[38] He brought the title, Mother of the Church, into prominence during the Council in 1964. Then in 1975, a votive Mass for Our Lady as Mother of the Church was added to the liturgy. Early in the pontificate of Pope John Paul II a young seminarian asked the Pope why there was no image of the Blessed Virgin Mary in St Peter's Square. That got the Pope thinking. Then in 1981, when shot by an assassin in St Peter's Square, he was miraculously saved through the intercession of Our Lady. In gratitude, he erected an image of Mary as Mother of the Church in a prominent corner to the right of the main facade. In his encyclical *Redemptoris Mater,* he also showed his support for the title.[39] Then in 2019, Pope Francis included the yearly feast of Mary the Mother of the Church in the Roman calendar on the Monday after Pentecost Sunday. Why is all of this so significant?

Pope Francis, following from Paul VI, sees Mary as a mother of tender love as she cares for the Church and helps us to appreciate the Church as our mother also. Mary is a figure or a mirror of the Church, which is made up of all the baptised.[40] In the Scriptures Mary is not spoken of as "Lady" or "Queen", but as the "mother of Jesus". This is an expression of tenderness. She was the first to behold the face of Jesus, the incarnate Son of God. She gazed upon God's face in the visage of her human son. One of the most touching icons of the Virgin Mary in the Byzantine tradition is the one called "Mother of tenderness". The face of the child Jesus is resting, cheek on cheek, against his mother's. The child is gazing at his mother and she is looking at us, almost as if to mirror the tenderness of God who came down to her from heaven and was incarnate in the Son, whom she holds in her arms. As we contemplate upon this image we can sense the wonderful love and mercy of God who so willingly gave his only Son (cf. Jn 3:16). But the icon also shows us, in Mary, the face of the Church through which the good news reaches every person. This icon has often drawn my heart into deeper union with God and awareness of his all-embracing love. I deliberately chose this image of our mother of tenderness to be on the front page of this book.

Pope Francis likes to remind us that the Church of all the baptised is feminine. The Church is a mother. If this identity were lost, the Church would become more like a charitable organisation, a football team or some social club. It would not bear abundant fruit in the Spirit. He proclaims the fundamental identity of the communion of the baptised is feminine – actively receptive to the work of the Spirit, full of tenderness and mercy, always giving of oneself in self-sacrificing service.

The apostolic line of bishops and priests is necessarily masculine. That is God's plan. But if the church was only that line, or even dominated in spirit by that line, it would be "a Church of old bachelors"![41] It would lose its fecundity and fail to engender the tenderness, which is in the heart of God. Mary, who is the mother of the Church helps us to understand this feminine dimension of the Church. The Church, he says is a woman, and has the attitude of a bride and mother. If we forget this we become "isolated, incapable of love and lacking in fruitfulness".[42] The Pope stresses that tenderness is the most characteristic quality of a woman. This is the motherly instinct and it is fundamental to the Church's identity.

Mary cradled her son in her arms, wrapped him in swaddling clothes and laid him in a manger. She knows the wisdom of the language of caresses, of silence, of the compassionate gaze. We all are called to learn from the genius of woman, which is so paramount in the Blessed Virgin Mary. This means attention to the individual person and his or her particular needs; not only fascinated with structures and systems, aiming to achieve outcomes and facilitate strategic goals, but attending to the needs of the person. A member of the Church must go along the same path as a mother – being a person who is gentle, tender, smiling and full of love. Pope John Paul II had drawn attention to this quality of women in his Letter to Women:

> Perhaps more than men, women acknowledge the person, because they see persons with their hearts. They see them independently of various ideological or political systems. They see others in their greatness and limitations; they try to go out to them and help them. In this way the basic plan of the Creator takes flesh in the history of humanity and there is constantly revealed, in the variety of vocations, that beauty – not merely physical, but above all spiritual – which God bestowed from the beginning on all, and in a particular way on women.[43]

Mary knows the language of tenderness and mercy. She protects the weak and is refuge for sinners. Without Mary, the woman, the Church does not go ahead because the Church also is a woman. This attitude of a woman comes to her from Mary, because Jesus wanted it that way. Both John Paul II and Francis emphasise the complementarity between the male and female characteristics in the Church. They are not polar opposites or in competition with one another. The church has a masculine, or Petrine, dimension, expressed in the apostolic line of bishops and priests. However, the Church is more fundamentally feminine. All of the baptised share in this Marian dimension. Consequently, it is most likely that we would be impoverished as a church if women are not empowered to be who they are and bring their "feminine genius" into the whole life of the Church. Mary is the exemplar, par excellence, for women to undertake this role of loving animation and tenderizing of the Church. A touching expression of this from a woman of faith is worth quoting:

> Why do we need Mary? We need Mary because as mother for all believers she humanises us and tenderises us, and makes us more welcoming of Christ. She teaches us in flesh and blood what it means to be a Christ-bearer – one who receives the Word, believes the Word, conceives the Word, and gives birth to him in a broken sinful world. Furthermore, she shows us how to persevere in suffering, and her intercession helps us to stand steady before it, especially before suffering that involves our children. For Mary, of all women, understands intimately how a mother is cut to the heart when she sees her offspring hurting.[44]

Mary for Men

The roles of men and women in the Church are meant to be complementary. Obviously, the apostolic dimension of the Church made up of bishops and priests, is necessarily male. However, it requires healthy collaboration with women in leadership for it to function well. Mary's motherly role means the feminine genius needs to influence high levels of governance in the Church.

Taking this issue further, we might well ask: what about the lay men in the Church? Does this image of Mary as mother, and hence the Church as mother, give the impression that the Church is mainly about women, with no clear role for men, apart from the clergy? Surely, the Blessed Virgin Mary would not want to give that impression. While inspiring women to their full potential as disciples of Jesus, she also calls lay men to take up their God-given responsibility in imitation of Christ.

Unfortunately, within the Church today, active lay men are a disappearing breed. Those relatively few men who are found in the pews can too often remain passive and disconnected, abdicating their responsibility to offer their unique gifting in leadership. Mary calls men to battle as warriors for Christ.[45] With the current widespread loss of faith, Catholic men are called to "step into the breach" – to fill the gap that lies open and vulnerable to further attack. They will need to grow in the "feminine" dimension of their heart in meeting people with tenderness and compassion, and bringing healing through a listening heart. But they will also need to grow in self-mastery, and use their God-given courage for adventure to break into new territory in evangelisation and unashamedly call others to Christ.

Men find Mary's presence in their lives a healing influence for any sexual brokenness, and a liberation from what has been called "toxic masculinity". Genuine manhood is synonymous with Christ-likeness. Just as Mary, together with Joseph, had a strong hand in forming Jesus towards manhood, she also desires men in the Church to stand up and follow Jesus courageously in the mission that is before us. She is keen to make sure each man, like Jesus growing up in Nazareth, has a "Joseph" in his life who can model to him true manhood and call him forward into what it means to be a man according to the way of Jesus. Yes, the Church is a mother for us all, but this image is not meant to emasculate men, but to encourage them to become fully themselves, complementing the role of women, and hence bringing the Church to her fullness intended by God.

The Miracle of Our Lady of Fatima

On 13 May 1981, near the start of his weekly general audience, as he was passing through St Peter's Square, Pope John Paul II was shot and seriously wounded by an assailant named Mehmet Ali Agca. In a critical condition, the Pope lay between life and death for some time in the Gemelli hospital. Shock waves went around the world as people prayed for his survival. Thankfully, the Pope rallied and was saved from death. At the moment the bullet hit the Pope's chest he cried out to the Blessed Mother. It was the feast day of Our Lady of Fatima. After his recovery the Pope expressed his conviction that it was "a motherly hand which guided the bullet's path", enabling "the dying Pope" to halt "at the threshold of death".[46] When a year later the Bishop of Fatima was visiting Rome the Pope gave him the bullet as a gift to be kept at the shrine. The bullet was later set in the crown of the statue of Our Lady of Fatima as a sign of God's protection over all who love his mother.

This assassination attempt on John Paul II prompted him to read again the so-called "third secret" of Fatima, and to ponder its significance. Unlike the earlier secrets, it had never been made public. However, it was not until the end of the twentieth century that he authorised the Congregation for Doctrine and Faith to reveal the contents of the secret. But before commenting any further on that, we should briefly describe the miracle of Fatima itself.[47] On 13 May 1917, three children who had taken the family flock of sheep to graze were startled by an apparition of a "most beautiful young woman". She asked them to come to this same spot at noon on the 13th of every month until October. This was noon solar time. They were poor peasants with no watches but knew how to gauge the time of day instinctively. The eldest of the children, Lucia Santos, was only 10. Her two younger companions were Francisco and Jacinta. The children experienced determined opposition from their families who thought Satan was deluding them. Their parish priest threatened them with punishment. Civil authorities persecuted them. However, the children calmly persisted in their seemingly outrageous claim.

Portugal at that time was in the throes of anti-Catholic persecution. The uprising was similar to that in the French revolution – anti-monarchy and anti-Catholic. By 1910 the new Republican government had disbanded the Jesuits and other religious orders, imprisoned leading clergy, confiscated church property and tried to govern all preaching and teaching in the parishes. Clerical attire was forbidden. While some of the hostility was anti-clerical, it was also a political program to abolish the Catholic Church as such, all in the name of rationalism and debunking anything supernatural. Now these three ignorant children were claiming to have supernatural visitations, and many people were gathering for the spectacle. The Lady in the apparition confided with the children three secrets. But her main message was one of repentance from sin and the need to turn back to God before it is too late. She told the children that on 13 October there would be a sign, which would show the unbelievers what the children were experiencing was real.

On the morning of 13 October it was raining. However, this did not deter a crowd of about 70,000 people gathering at the Cova da Iria where the apparitions had been occurring. During the preceding six months, newspapers and periodicals had spread the news of the strange things happening and in particular of the prediction of a major miracle on this day. There were many believers with expectant hearts, but also unbelievers, who had come to mock and deride when nothing happened. One rude cartoon in the popular press had as a caption: the only "apparition" would be the very real hunger of the impoverished! At noon, the children went into an ecstatic state. Lucia yelled out, "Put down your umbrellas!" and then "Look at the sun!" People looked upwards to see the rain had ceased, clouds had parted, and the sun appeared shining brilliantly. For the next 10 to 12 minutes, witnesses said, "The sun began to dance". It whirled around like a Catherine wheel firecracker. Then it zigzagged erratically across the sky. Then it seemed to be heading towards earth, but continued to dance. Everyone, both believer and unbeliever saw this amazing phenomenon. No scientific explanation was possible. It was purely a spectacular supernatural event.

Let us now return to the secrets of Fatima.[48] The first secret given to the children was a vision of hell, which they described in vivid detail. It was a warning that it is a narrow gate that leads to salvation and only a few take it; while it is a broad and spacious path that leads to damnation and many take it. Mary taught the children to add to the Rosary the prayer, "O my Jesus, forgive us our sins. Save us from the fires of hell. Bring all souls to heaven, especially those who most need your mercy". The second secret was the prediction of World War II and the emergence of Russian domination. With this came the call to pray for the conversion of Russia. The Pope was to consecrate the whole world to the Immaculate Heart of Mary. These messages had already been made public. But, as mentioned earlier, the third secret was not made public until the year 2000.

In making these secrets public, the Church was careful to remind us that they are "private revelations" and so it is not necessary to believe them. Cardinal Ratzinger, later Pope Benedict XVI, described them as prophecies, which call us to a sharper living of the fundamental gospel message. Prophecy in the biblical sense is not so much about predicting the future, but aims to "explain the will of God for the present, and therefore show the right path to take for the future".[49] While the prophecies of Fatima did have a predictive element he emphasised that they are really meant to shake us out of apathy and call us back to a radical living of the gospel as genuine disciples of Jesus. The third secret then was an extended image-laden prophecy. An angel with a flaming sword was crying out, "Penance, penance, penance!" There was a large crowd of people and "a Bishop dressed in white" which the children thought was the Holy Father. They were all ascending a steep mountain towards a big, rough-hewn Cross. Along the way, there were many corpses. When the Holy Father reached the top of the mountain, he was shot dead by soldiers and with him other bishops, priests, religious and lay people. The blood of the martyrs was being gathered by the angels and they were sprinkling it on those making their way to God.

This prophecy was apt for the twentieth century in which more martyrs died for the faith than in the whole previous history of the church. And, when Pope John Paul II was shot, he was no doubt saved by the prayers of the faithful and especially those of the Blessed Virgin Mary. After the near death experience in 1981, Pope John Paul II felt free to reveal the prophecy and give thanks to the Blessed Virgin who averted the disaster, which threatened him on her feast day. He also made sure that he followed the Virgin's instructions and consecrated Russia and the whole world to the Immaculate Heart of Mary. Only a few years later, the Berlin Wall fell and the USSR broke into independent states. The cold war was over.

8

MOTHER WHO INTERCEDES FOR US

Mary is given to us by Jesus to be our mother. Now that she is glorified, she has not forgotten us. Just like Esther, who did not forget her own people after she became queen, neither does Mary forget us. When Esther's people were in danger of being exterminated Esther took her life into her hands and begged the king to change his heart. She stood for her people and interceded for them (Esther 5:1-17). Our Blessed Mother, who is now Queen of heaven and earth, intercedes for us also. This is the primary way she cares for us. She is not herself the source of grace. Her place is one of humble intercession for God to give us grace. However, her intercession is always effective. Why? Because Jesus promised that we would receive anything asked of him that is according to his will (1Jn 4:6). Mary only asks for what is according to God's will. She desires everything God wants. When she asks, God does what she desires. In this way, she cooperates with God's work on earth.

We are familiar with the famous words of Therese of Lisieux when she was dying. As a young Carmelite, she had given herself totally to intercessory prayer for the lost. Now when she is about to go to God she says:

> I feel that my mission is about to begin; my mission of making souls love the good God as I love him, to teach my little way to souls. If my desires receive fulfilment, I shall spend my heaven on earth even until the end of time. Yes, I will spend my heaven doing good upon earth.[50]

Therese is espousing Mary's vocation for her continuing mission on earth and making it her own. That is what Mary is doing for all eternity; interceding for her children who are struggling in their earthly pilgrimage. But Mary's intercession is of a uniquely powerful kind, beyond what other saintly figures may provide. We need to explore this further.

The incident at Cana in Galilee presented in John's gospel provides an initial revelation of Mary's maternal intercessory care for all humanity. It speaks to us of her solicitude for all who are in need. In this case, the need was relatively minor, although a significant embarrassment for the recently married couple. Mary notices their need immediately and goes to her Son. "They have no wine". She does not act herself but brings the need to her Son relying on his salvific power. It is the first indication of Mary's role in mediation, placing herself between her Son and the desires, needs and suffering of humanity. She is confident that through her mysterious intimacy with her Son that he will not leave her request unmet. It is the first revelation of Mary's intercessory role for the world. She simply tells the servants, "Do whatever he tells you". Here Mary is showing her utmost belief in Jesus and confidence in his power to act. We can see that she really wants his messianic power to be manifest.

The early Fathers of the Church were keen to point out that Mary's role in the salvation of the world was not merely passive. Through her faith and obedience, she cooperated in the work of human salvation. St Irenaeus proclaimed that being obedient she "became the cause of salvation for herself and the whole human race".[51] This does not mean she made it happen. Rather, she was the willing instrument God used to make it happen. Her whole pilgrim journey, from the moment of her consent in Nazareth to the yielding of her will to God as she stood at the foot of the Cross, was a sharing in the work of salvation. The Vatican Council II explains, "In a wholly singular way she cooperated by her obedience, faith, hope and burning charity in the work of the Saviour in restoring supernatural life to souls. For this reason she is a mother to us in the order of grace".[52] However, it is important not to attribute to Mary what is properly the work of Jesus. Her role in the redemption of the world was totally subordinate to that of Jesus and totally dependent on the merits of Christ's sacrifice on the Cross and glorious resurrection.

Now that Mary has entered into glory her intercession has become so much more powerful and universal in scope. Although it depends totally upon what Jesus accomplished for us on the Cross and through his glorious resurrection. While she was Mother of God on earth, her life was hidden and full of self-denial. Now she has been assumed bodily into heaven she shares in the glorious resurrection of Jesus, and all the graces of salvation flowing from his redemption of humanity. She is Queen of heaven and earth. When she was assumed into heaven, Mary did not relinquish her saving role, but "by her manifold intercession continues to bring us the gifts of eternal salvation".[53] She continues to intercede for us in times of sorrow, misfortune, anxiety, and spiritual battle. She does not act as an outsider, but as one of us, who has a unique place in our lives and in the life of the Church, as our mother.

In the words of Vatican II,

> Mary's maternal function towards mankind in no way obscures or diminishes the unique mediation of Christ, but rather shows its efficacy because 'there is one mediator between God and man, the man Christ Jesus (1 Tim 2:5).[54]

Her mediation is always "in Christ". She now enjoys total union with God, so any action of hers cannot be done apart from God. The Council expressed it well:

> The Blessed Virgin's salutary influence on men originates not in any inner necessity but in the disposition of God. It flows forth from the superabundance of the merits of Christ, rests

on his mediation, depends entirely upon it and draws all its power from it.[55]

So calling upon Mary to intercede for us does not impede our immediate union with Christ. Rather it fosters this union. It is not a choice between Mary or Christ! Turning to the Blessed Virgin Mary will always take us deeper into Christ and the power of his saving love. If it does not then it is a perverted form of Marian devotion, which does not give glory to God.

Mary's mediation is a sharing in the one unique source of our salvation, Jesus our Redeemer. Her mediation is subordinate to Christ.[56] She is a creature and cannot be classed as equal with Jesus, who is the Incarnate Word and Redeemer of humankind. Her effectiveness in the world depends totally on the saving power of her Son. She lives in him at all times, sharing totally in the life of the Trinity. The power of her intercession is due to her intimacy with her Son and submission to his will.

All disciples of Jesus are encouraged to intercede for one another, and in that way we share in the one mediation of Christ. It is a standard practice in the Church to approach someone we consider close to the Lord to pray for us. This is particularly with those who have gone before us to heaven and are recognised by the Church as canonised saints. However, Mary, who is Queen of all saints, is intercessor in a singularly unique way.

Mary's share in the one mediation of Christ is special, extraordinary and universal. Let us look at each of these qualities. It is *special* because her intimacy with Christ is unique; this means her mediation between God and humanity is in a league of its own. It is an *extraordinary* mediation since she is "full of grace", surrendered totally to the will of God, and has become for all people, "mother in the order of grace". Mary's place in heaven is exceptional due to the way she was chosen to cooperate with God's salvation of the world. She continues this work as "handmaid of the Lord" forever in heaven. Furthermore, Mary's intercession, unlike that of others, is *universal* in extent, because the work of redemption embraces all humanity. Her unique cooperation in the salvation of the world as Mother of the Saviour, means that her mediation of grace through her intercession now is effective for all men and women.

A Mother's Heart of Mercy

The Blessed Virgin Mary has a mother's heart for every human being, and especially for those who are most desperate. She is Mother of Mercy. She has been instrumental in millions of people being rescued from their plight and coming to know and love God. Stories of conversions through her intercession abound. One well attested story is that of Donald Calloway.[57] By the age of eight, he had three fathers. The last one adopted him and gave him his name. As a teenager in San Diego, he became hopelessly promiscuous. When the family moved to Japan, he joined a criminal gang. At the age of 17, he was addicted to illegal substances and became a drug mule for the local "mafia". He was arrested and deported back to the United States and given over to the custody of his family. Meanwhile his mother had converted to the Catholic faith. She came to love Jesus, and found herself often asking Our Lady's intercession for her son's conversion.

Donald would disappear from the family home for weeks. Then he would find himself without money and a place to stay. He remembers, "Sometimes there was no one available who I could 'use' for food and shelter. In that situation I had no choice but to return home, just so I'd have something to eat and a place to sleep". His parents would always take him back, even though they were furious with his behaviour. As soon as he could arrange things, he would be off again couch-surfing, pursuing an indolent, destructive life-style.

During one of his brief stays at home, his mother suggested he might like to go to church with her. He just looked at her with a blank stare and replied, "Are you nuts? Me go to church? No way. Church is for the weak. It's for the losers who are looking for some false hope when there is none. Church is a joke and a lie. I can't believe you and dad have been suckered into believing this nonsense."

Donald's Mum never gave up on him. She held out hope that he would change. It was a hope grounded in the mercy of God and the intercession of our Blessed Mother. It was a hope in the power of God to heal a wounded heart and bring her druggie/hippie son to his senses. Many times she would cry herself to sleep begging the help of our Blessed Mother Mary. The whole family would pray for Donald trusting in God's mercy and Our Lady's intercession. Even though it seemed hopeless, she would not give up.

Her trust was not in vain. One night in March 1992, Donald was hit by what he calls a "Divine 4x2". For no clear reason he had decided to stay home in his room rather than go out partying with his friends. After a while, the stillness was too much for him. He needed a distraction. Perusing the bookshelf, he grabbed a book that would change his life. It was an account of apparitions of the Blessed Virgin Mary at Medjugorje. As he flipped through the book, he felt captivated by this figure called the "Blessed Virgin". He was intrigued with her and the message she was bringing. She was the mother to all and especially to sinners.

He also found a card in the book which read, "You don't have to change to love me; loving me will change you". And it did. He fell in love with Mary, his mother. She had captivated him with her love and tenderness. He later wrote:

> As I read, I knew I had to give myself to this thing Mary called 'church'. She always seemed to be leading or pointing towards it. I always imagined church as being oppressive, something that dominated your life and sucked all the fun out of life. I

believed that was the role of the Church, so naturally I hated church, just like I hated Jesus. But if I was going to surrender to Mary, I had to believe her and give myself to Jesus and the Church. And even though I didn't verbalise it or speak it internally, somehow I knew I had to surrender to this Blessed Virgin Mary. She would help me understand the real Jesus, the Jesus whom I never knew.[58]

By morning, he was convinced. "I have never ever heard anything so amazing and convincing and so needed in my life". He believed this Virgin Mary had come from heaven for him. He was desperate to tell his mum. Feeling deeply humiliated he stumbled in blurting out to her, "Mum, I've got to talk to a Catholic priest". His mother brushed it off, probably thinking he was just using another manipulative ploy. But he insisted. "No, Mum, you don't understand I read a book last night. That book is tripping me out!". "Which book?" she asked, looking quizzical. Donald ran to get the book and asked her point blank "Who is this Blessed Virgin Mary? What is this all about?"

Donald says, "At that point, my mum's jaw just about hit the floor. She didn't say another word. She ran to the phone in the living room and began dialling." She was calling priests at 6.00am in the morning! Not being very successful, they decided to go to a chapel close by. His conversion had begun. And the ultimate outcome many years later was even more astounding. Donald Calloway was ordained a Catholic priest in 2003 and has a ministry of preaching as he spreads the good news of God's mercy, which he experienced so profoundly through the intercession of Our Lady of Mercy.

The Rosary as Intercession

I have already indicated how the Rosary is a means of allowing Mary to take us more into the mystery of Christ, and to contemplate more deeply his love for us. It is also a powerful means of intercession.

Australia has been consecrated to Our Lady under the title of "Help of Christians". The origin of the title is connected to the Rosary as a powerful means of finding victory.[59] In 1571, Christian Europe came under attack from a giant Islamic naval armada, which attempted to land in the Gulf of Lepanto, near the Greek coastal city of Corinth. This was a major threat to the existence of Christianity. In history, there have been very few battles as decisive as this one.

The Christian fleet under the leadership of Don John of Austria seemed to be no match for the strength of the attacking enemy. The fate of Christianity hung on the outcome of the battle. The Pope, St Pius V, entrusted the outcome to the help of Our Lady and ordered uninterrupted prayers to Our Lady during the battle. Rosary processions thronged the streets of Europe and the Pope prayed with outstretched arms in his oratory on Vatican Hill. The battle was fierce and casualties on both sides were in the thousands. But the victory came. The mighty Turk Armada was routed. Christians hailed Our Lady's intercession, which had miraculously turned the tide of history against impossible odds. The date was 7 October 1571. That is why the Church to this day celebrates Our Lady of the Rosary on that day each year. From that time onwards, the title "Help of Christians" became popular for Mary.

Fr John Therry, the first priest in Australia was ordained a priest in 1814, the year that Pope Pius VII had been released from prison. The Pope had been incarcerated by Napoleon and treated with cruelty and humiliation for five years. He had appealed to Christians to pray to Our Lady Help of Christians. The Rosary was prayed throughout Europe. Napoleon was eventually forced by the military to release the Pope, and on 24th May 1814 the Pope made his triumphal return to Rome. That is why 24 May was from that time onwards the feast of Our Lady Help of Christians. Fr Therry, having been ordained in that momentous year, had a strong devotion to Mary under that title. So in 1821 when the Cathedral in Sydney had its foundation stone laid, it was dedicated to "Mary, Immaculate Mother, Help of Christians". In 1841, Fr Therry wrote to Archbishop Polding requesting that Australia be dedicated to Our Lady Help of Christians. This happened in a Synod in 1844 and was approved by Rome in 1852. On 24 May 2001, the Centenary of Federation, the bishops of Australia gathered in St Mary's Cathedral to solemnly rededicate Australia to Our Lady Help of Christians. She is patroness of this great country.

The Rosary then is a powerful weapon in spiritual warfare. As Paul says, "it is not against human enemies that we have to struggle, but against the sovereignties and the powers who originate the darkness in this world, the spiritual army of evil in the heavens" (Eph 6:12). The armour we must wear and the weapons we must use need to come from God. Otherwise, we will not have the power to resist, nor the resources to hold our ground. The testimony of the ages is that the Rosary is such a weapon. Paul encourages us, "Pray all the time, asking what you need, praying in the Spirit on every possible occasion. Never get tired of staying awake to pray for all the saints" (Eph 6:18). The Rosary is a great means of claiming the victory of Jesus in the midst of the battle. But not only the Rosary. At all times, no matter what the manner of our prayer, we can invoke the help of the Blessed Virgin Mary, who will always come to our aid.

Good News out of Africa

Bishop Oliver Doeme Dashe of Maiduguri Diocese in north-eastern Nigeria has a story that has kept people in the West spellbound.[60] In that part of Nigeria, the Boko Haram have been harassing the Church and killing almost indiscriminately. This Islamic terrorist group has murdered thousands and caused half a million people to be displaced. Recruiting illiterate boys as "child soldiers" they radicalise them and promise them riches if they murder, and heaven if they lose their life doing so. They abduct young girls to sell them on the market as "child brides", or use them for themselves. At one stage, 2,000 girls were in custody of the Boko Haram.

In the Bishop's diocese, a seminary was looted and destroyed, churches damaged, 20 schools sacked, and five convents burnt to the ground. The message of the Boko Haram is "convert to Islam or die". Bishop Oliver had no way of responding to this crisis, but to turn to prayer. He encouraged his people to call upon Our Lady's help. He consecrated his diocese to the Immaculate Heart of Mary, declared a year of Our Lady, and many parishes engaged in regular Rosary processions. Then one day in 2014, when he was praying the Rosary before the exposed Blessed Sacrament in his private chapel, Jesus appeared to him. Jesus said nothing, but he was holding a large sword of shining steel. He held out the sword to the Bishop, who reached out to take this weapon. As he took hold of the sword, it turned into Rosary beads! Jesus said, "Boko Haram is finished! Boko Haram is finished! Boko Haram is finished!" Immediately Bishop Oliver knew what this meant. The Lord was giving him a sword of unbelievable power. He was affirming the Rosary, which his diocese had been faithfully praying, as the best weapon against their enemy. The demonic work of Boko Haram could only be overcome through Mary's prayers. She, who has crushed the head of the serpent will, through her intercession bring the victory of Jesus over the powers of Satan.

Bishop Oliver shared this vision with his priests and then with all of his people. They took heart; their prayers would be answered; they would be set free from fear, danger and oppression. Three years later the Boko Haram had been almost eliminated from his diocese. The Nigerian military have taken control of the region, and the task of rebuilding is before them.

Blessed Bartolo Longo

Bartolo Longo was dubbed the "Apostle of the Rosary" by Pope John

Paul II. This was amazing since Bartolo had been a Satanist priest before he discovered the power of the Rosary.[61] He was born in 1841 into a devout Catholic family near Brindisi, Italy. He was a smart but mischievous kid. The loss of his mother at the age of ten caused deep trauma. Then in his teenage years, he was influenced by the anti-Catholic feeling abroad. By the time he entered University in Naples many of his teachers were disenchanted ex-priests preaching against the Church. He recalls, "I, too, grew to hate monks, priests and the Pope". He had a particular disdain for the Dominicans who were the most vocal opponents of his professors. A new "freedom" was in the air. He rejected God and began to visit mediums. Drawn by the occult, thirsting for meaning in something supernatural, he entered Satanism. After a rigorous initiation, he was consecrated as a satanic priest and promised his soul to the devil. He preached vehemently against God and the Church, seeing them as the real evils.

His family could not call him to his senses. However, a Catholic professor at the university befriended him. He warned Bartolo that he could end up in an insane asylum if he kept going the way he was heading. Bartolo couldn't deny that his physiological and psychological state was sadly deteriorating. Professor Pepe eventually convinced him to see a Dominican priest. After three weeks of protracted conversations, he decided to return to the Church. On the feast of the Sacred Heart in 1865, he received absolution and returned to communion with the Church. However, he was still hounded by the guilt of his liaison with the devil. Having taken up praying the Rosary, he found peace in its rhythm and spiritual protection.

As a voluntary penance he worked in the Hospital for Incurables, and prayed unceasingly. He made a promise of celibacy and became a Third Order Dominican. The Rosary became his solace and his protection from Satan. He would courageously return to his old Satanist haunts, hold up his Rosary beads and publicly renounce his former ways. He was already experiencing the comfort of the presence of the Blessed Mother. Yet he still found it hard to forgive himself. He was plagued with guilt and still wondered whether he could be saved.

Peace came to his soul when on a visit to Pompeii. Feeling torn apart in his heart by his dark past, he remembered the voice of a Dominican Friar who had repeated the words of the Blessed Virgin Mary, "The one who propagates my Rosary shall be saved". This became his mission. He spent the rest of his life propagating the Rosary and seeking to imitate the mysteries it contained.

Bartolo's life was transformed by the Blessed Virgin Mary and the Rosary. He founded schools and orphanages, built a Cathedral in Pompeii to Our Lady of the Rosary, started a printing business and technical school to give children of convicted criminals a way out of poverty. He became friends with Pope Leo XIII who also had a deep devotion to the Rosary. But his most lasting legacy was the luminous mysteries of the Rosary. It was from Bartolo's writings that Pope John Paul II gained the inspiration to include these mysteries of the ministry of Jesus in the Rosary.

At the end of his Apostolic Letter on the Rosary Pope John Paul II disclosed that he makes his own the beautiful prayer of Blessed Bartolo. We could make it our own as well:

> O Blessed Rosary of Mary, sweet chain which unites us to God, bond of love which unites us to the angels, tower of salvation against the assaults of Hell, safe port in our universal shipwreck, we will never abandon you. You will be our comfort in the hour of death: yours our final kiss as life ebbs away. And the last word from our lips will be your sweet name, O Queen of the Rosary, O dearest Mother, O Refuge of Sinners, O Sovereign Consoler of the Afflicted. May you be everywhere blessed, today and always, on earth and in heaven.[62]

PART III

MARY AND THE HOLY SPIRIT

9

MARY AND PENTECOST

From the moment of her conception, Mary was sanctified by the Holy Spirit. The angel Gabriel greeted her as "full of grace". From the beginning of her earthly journey, she enjoyed the indwelling presence of sanctifying grace without any taint of sin. The Holy Spirit dwelt within her in a measure far greater than any other creature who becomes a child of God through baptism. Vatican II declared that she was the "sanctuary of the Holy Spirit; an exceptional gift of grace placing her far above other creatures in heaven and on earth".[63] She is radiant with the Spirit, totally transparent with the Spirit, and completely docile to the Spirit.

Annunciation and Pentecost

Even though she possessed the Holy Spirit from the beginning, we know from Luke's gospel and Acts of the Apostles that there were two major moments in which she experienced new anointings of the Spirit – at the Annunciation and at Pentecost. The life of holiness, even in one as perfect as the Blessed Virgin Mary, was not static and frozen as if she was a statue. It was a lived reality as circumstances and challenges in life unfolded in unexpected ways. Before each crisis in our lives there is new grace made for the call of the moment. That is how it was with the Blessed Virgin Mary also. Her journey was profoundly human, but filled with grace in ever new and deeper ways.

We can draw a parallel between the Annunciation and Pentecost. Most likely, this was intended by Luke who wrote both his gospel and Acts. Of all the evangelists, he gives special attention to the Holy Spirit and Mary. At the Annunciation through the outpouring of the Holy Spirit Mary became the mother of Christ. In the Upper room at Pentecost through the fire of the Spirit, she became the mother of the Church.

When Gabriel announced to Mary she was to be the mother of the Messiah, Mary questioned, "But how can this come about, since I do not know man?" She was told, "The Holy Spirit will come upon you and you will be overshadowed by God the Most High" (Lk 1:35). This is a reference to the "shekinah" glory of God, which filled the Temple of old. Now Mary is the new Temple to be filled with the glory of God. She was to be the new "Ark of the Covenant", not housing manna, commandments and staff, but the eternal Son of God. That is how the impossible would happen. That is how the incarnation would take place. The Holy Spirit would create, sanctify and unite the humanity of Jesus to his Divinity within her very womb. By the power of the Holy Spirit, the word made flesh was conceived. The Spirit brought forth Jesus in the Virgin's womb. Then by the power of the Spirit Mary brought Jesus to the world.

The Annunciation for Mary was a threshold moment in her journey. She realised even more acutely the power of the sanctifying presence of the Holy Spirit in her life and became ever more docile to the movement of the Spirit and expectant of the Spirit's activity. Her "yes' – "let it be done to me"- gave free reign to the Holy Spirit to do his transforming work at every moment of her earthly journey. With the Holy Spirit coming upon her she was progressively given deeper insight into the role she was to play in the work of redemption. She was overwhelmed by the immense love of God, allowing herself to be sanctified and strengthened to live in a fully committed way the new vocation given to her.

What happened at Pentecost was another decisive moment. Mary was gathered with the apostles and many others in the Upper Room because they had been told by Jesus, "You will receive power when the Holy Spirit comes on you and then you will be my witnesses" (Acts 1:8). Here Mary is in the midst of the first disciples as the poorest and most humble of all, imploring for the Spirit to come in unceasing prayer. Again, power comes from on high. There was a mighty wind and the whole place shook, and then tongues of fire settled on each of them and they began to speak in tongues and prophesy. This charismatic awakening was a new dimension to her experience of the Spirit, due to her openness and also those who were with her, obediently waiting upon "power from on high" (Lk 24:49). Here was another birthing happening. The Church was born in the Spirit. The Spirit gives boldness to preach, heal and deliver in the name of Jesus. From this "womb", by the power of the Spirit many would be born in Christ. Mary continues now and always to pray at the heart of the Church for its rebirthing. She brings Jesus to the hearts of all to whom the gospel is preached, birthing them in faith and new life in God.

At the Annunciation, the Holy Spirit came upon Mary for the birthing of the word made flesh, the Christ. At Pentecost, the Holy Spirit came upon Mary for the birthing of the Church, the Body of Christ. In the first instance, she became the mother of Christ; in the second, she became the mother of the Church. The Spirit overshadowing Mary at the Annunciation made it possible for her to bring Christ to the world. The Spirit poured out at Pentecost upon those gathered with Mary in their midst, made it possible for Mary to begin her role as mother of the Church. She participates in the Holy Spirit's action in birthing new Christians in faith and new life in God. Mary now continues to pray at the heart of the Church for its perpetual rebirthing.

Praying for a Perpetual Pentecost

What does Mary teach us by her presence in the Cenacle at the moment of Pentecost? What was significant about her powerful presence in the community gathered? In Acts, Jesus had instructed the apostles not to leave Jerusalem but to wait expectantly to be "baptised in the Holy Spirit" (Acts 1:4-5). Luke's gospel also ends with this instruction: "Stay in the city, until you are clothed with power from on high" (Lk 24:29). Perseverance in prayer was critical for Pentecost to happen. In obedience, the apostles went to Jerusalem and gathered in the upper room where they were staying. They "joined in continuous prayer, together with several women, including Mary the mother of Jesus and with his brothers" (Acts 1:14). Mary's presence is highlighted. She is called the "mother of Jesus", which gives her particular focus in the community. They prayed in one accord, and, most significantly, they prayed with perseverance.

The pattern of Pentecost is meant to be the ongoing pattern of the Church. We are meant to be experiencing a perpetual Pentecost. How can this happen? The answer is by persevering prayer for the Holy Spirit in union with Mary, mother of the Church. At the first Pentecost Mary, the apostles and others formed one heart of supplication for the Holy Spirit. It is a prayer made with one accord. St Augustine said, "If therefore, you wish to receive the Holy Spirit, keep charity and desire unity".[64]

The fundamental and constant prayer of the Church is "Come, Holy Spirit". This persevering prayer means we ask often, never ceasing to hope, never giving up. Jesus himself promised the Holy Spirit would be given if we ask; "if you then, who are evil, know how to give good gifts to your children, how much more will the heavenly father give the Holy Spirit to those who ask him!" (Lk 11:13) The bestowal of the gift of the Spirit comes as a result of prayer. It is not that God is bound only to give the Spirit when we ask. But is it clear that the best way to open ourselves and others to this gift is through persevering prayer.

In Acts again and again the apostles' prayer invokes the Holy Spirit. After Peter and John had been arrested and released, the community was praying: "As they prayed, the house where they were assembled rocked: they were all filled with the Holy Spirit and began to proclaim the word of God boldly" (Acts 4:31). When the apostles heard that Samaria had received the word of God, they sent Peter and John, who "came down and prayed for them that they might receive the Holy Spirit" (Acts 8:15). Saul was praying after his Damascus experience when the Lord sent him Ananias so he may regain his sight and be filled with the Spirit (Acts 9:9-11). Peter was praying when he was told to go to Cornelius' house and preach so that the gentiles may also receive the gift of the Spirit (Acts 11:44). I suggest the primary role of the Blessed Mother in the Church after Pentecost, and even more so after being assumed and glorified with the Risen Jesus, is to persevere in prayer for the Holy Spirit. She teaches us to join her in this as the Church's mission goes forward and people's hearts are opened to the Lord.

All of the Church's work and mission gains its power from the Holy Spirit. Otherwise, we are trying to engage in a supernatural mission with natural means. As the Fourth Assembly of the World Council of Churches stated so pointedly in the Uppsala Report:

> Without the Holy Spirit: God is far away, Christ stays in the past, the Gospel is a dead letter, the Church is simply an organisation, authority a matter of domination, mission a matter of propaganda, liturgy no more than evocation, Christian living a slave morality.
>
> But with the Holy Spirit: the cosmos is resurrected and groans with the birth-pangs of the Kingdom, the risen Christ is there, the Gospel is the power of life, the Church shows forth the life of the Trinity, authority is liberating service, mission is a Pentecost, the liturgy is both memorial and anticipation, human action is deified.[65]

Mother Mary shows us the way of persevering prayer for the coming of the Spirit. Otherwise, the Church will stagnate and lose its youthfulness. With the Holy Spirit we are forever new, forever creative, forever fresh and vigorous in our proclamation and forever eager for the salvation of others. What happened at Pentecost was a repetition of the power of the Holy Spirit coming upon Jesus when he was baptised in the Jordan. Luke is keen to let us know that it was precisely as Jesus was praying that "the heavens opened and the Holy Spirit descended upon him" (Lk 3:21-22). It was the prayer of Jesus that rent the heavens and brought down the Holy Spirit upon him. The same thing happened for the Church at Pentecost when Mary and the apostles were praying. This needs to happen continually through ongoing invocation of the Spirit with Mary in our midst.

Mary and Holy Spirit in John's Gospel

In John's gospel, we find a different account of Pentecost, but just as important. Again, the Blessed Virgin Mary is present. Firstly, we need to understand why there are two versions of Pentecost. For John, the outpouring of the Spirit belongs to the Easter experience of Jesus' glorification through his death and resurrection. Whereas, for Luke, Pentecost occurs 50 days after Easter following a prolonged period of intense prayer. The latter style has prevailed in the way we celebrate liturgically. But from earliest days there has been two different perspectives. Rather than try to combine them, it is best to draw from each account the fullness of what each author intended. In Luke's account, the Holy Spirit is poured out for mission, empowering with gifts to enable the preaching of the gospel to go forward. In John's account, the Spirit is given for interior transformation; rather than for charismatic gifts, the Spirit is given for sanctifying the individual.

The high point of John's gospel is Jesus as King of love on Calvary. The legs of the two men crucified on either side of Jesus were broken to hasten death. We are told: "When they came to Jesus, they found he was already dead, and so instead of breaking his legs one of the soldiers pierced his side with a lance; and immediately there came out blood and water" (Jn 19:33-34). John understood the blood and water flowing from Jesus' side as fulfilment of the promise of living waters that would flow from his heart, and as a sign of the Spirit that those who believed in him would receive (Jn 7:37). The early Fathers saw the fountain of water from the side of Christ as a symbol of baptism. The Spirit being poured out from the pierced heart of Christ brings a new creation. The Spirit brings a new birth in Christ. "It is the Spirit which gives life" (Jn 6:63). The Holy Spirit changes us into the likeness of Jesus, helping us to abide in him and he in us (1Jn 4:13). So, in John's account the outpouring of the Spirit is not so much about charismatic gifts and wonders for mission, but rather about the sanctifying of the individual as a new creation in Christ.

What is most important for us, of course, is that Mary was present at this outpouring of the Spirit. After Jesus had given Mary to us and given us to Mary, he cried out "It is finished!" All that needed to be accomplished was done. As we saw earlier, this scene could also be called the birth of the Church. Mary, the mother of Jesus, and now the mother of all believers and John the Beloved disciple represent the Church. Mary, the daughter of Zion, predicted by the prophets, is the figure of the Church. Jesus, out of perfect love, constituted the Church as the people of God and gave them the gift of the Spirit. They were the first to be "baptised in the Spirit" beneath the Cross, representing the whole Church. This was the moment for John when God's gift was given to the world. The promise of the living spring was fulfilled.

This life-giving water from the side of Christ is foretold in the image given by Ezekiel of the spring arising in the Temple and flowing out to the desert, bringing fruitful vegetation wherever it goes (Ez 47:1ff). It is also a fulfilment of the prophecy when he spoke of the new covenant: "I will sprinkle clean water upon you…A new heart I will give you, and a new spirit I will put within you; and I will take out of your flesh the heart of stone and give you a heart of flesh. And I will put my spirit within you" (Ez 36:25-27). Jesus himself had given his promise of this living water: "If any man is thirsty, let him come to me! Let the man come and drink who believes in me". Jesus quotes the text, "From his breast shall flow fountains of living water". John tells us he was speaking of the Spirit which his believers were yet to receive "for there was no Spirit yet because Jesus had not yet been glorified" (Jn 7:37-39). At last, the life-giving water was poured out from his side opened on Calvary. The living water of the Holy Spirit comes to sanctify, to refresh, to renew, to bring personal transformation.

At the foot of the Cross, Mary was filled with the Spirit in a new way. Her great act of obedience beneath the Cross dilated her heart and made it possible for her to receive the Holy Spirit to an even greater degree. The more a person's heart expands in love the more capable they are of receiving a greater effusion of the Spirit. Mary was "fashioned by the Holy Spirit into a new creature".[66] This does not refer to her immaculate conception alone. Rather her acceptance and possession of the Holy Spirit grew throughout her life as her heart expanded in love and she became more capable of receiving more of the Spirit. The high point of this personal transformation was as she stood at the foot of the Cross. United with her Son in his agony, her heart was dilated in love, and she was fashioned into a new creature, capable of loving God with her whole heart and soul and mind.

Whereas in the Lukan Pentecost the emphasis is on the dramatic earthquake and fire from heaven, bringing signs and wonders and a new power for missionary preaching, John's emphasis is different. John focusses on how the Holy Spirit brings intimacy with God. The image of water as a spring welling up to eternal life, which Jesus promised the woman at the well, is an invitation to intimacy. The other image of John, which we have not yet mentioned, the breath of God, when he breathed on his apostles after the resurrection, also speaks of intimacy. In the ancient culture to breathe on another is an invitation to intimate union. The Spirit dwells in us so we can abide in Christ and he in us. Whereas the Lukan presentation is more missionary in focus, John's perspective is more contemplative. They complement one another.

Mary and the Holy Spirit at Medjugorje

When we speak about the Holy Spirit, we must speak about Mary, and when we speak about Mary, we cannot but speak of the Holy Spirit. On June 24th 1981 in a remote village in the former communist Yugoslavia, two teenage girls, Mirjana and Ivanka, went for a walk.[67] Ivanka suddenly noticed a light high up on Mount Podbrdo, the large rocky hill behind the village. Looking up she saw a woman hovering above the ground, holding a baby in her arms, and radiating light. She had blue eyes and long dark hair, dressed in a grey dress and a white veil, and a crown of twelve stars around her head. Both girls were dumbfounded. Then a friend Vicka came looking for them. She saw the woman also. She ran headlong back to the village. Then a few moments later, a teenage boy, Ivan, came by. When he saw the apparition, he dropped what he was carrying and ran away. The others followed, confused about what they had seen. The next day all four children felt drawn back to the same spot. Vicka brought along her friend Marija and ten-year old Jakov. All six of them saw the beautiful woman. The next day almost the entire village turned up and witnessed the children taken up into the company of the woman, but they could not themselves see her. Vicka's grandmother gave her some holy water and instructed her to sprinkle it on the apparition. She did so, saying, "If you are the devil, go away from us". The woman just smiled with immense love and spoke: "Do not be afraid, dear angels, I am the Mother of God. I am Queen of Peace. I am the mother of all people". Thus began the apparitions at Medjugorje, which have drawn millions to receive the blessing, and also have been surrounded with controversy from the beginning.

The official Church has not yet authenticated the Medjugorje apparitions, but encourages pilgrims to come to this little village with the double-spired Church of St James, the Apparition Hill, and the higher Mt Krisevac. The latter has become a focus of pilgrimage, especially with the Stations of the Cross. I first visited Medjugorje in 1984 with a friend who knew more about what was happening than I did. Arriving at a neighbouring village where acquaintances of my friend were providing hospitality, we noticed that, while they fed us well, the family themselves were not eating. It was Wednesday and Our Lady had asked the whole village to fast on bread and water on both Wednesdays and Fridays. At 5.00pm we were taken to the Church of St James, and because we were priests, we were showed into the sacristy. It was full of people on their knees, as was the whole church, while the assembly was praying the rosary.

I looked around somewhat inquisitively and noticed next to me six young children. "Who are they?" I asked my friend. "The visionaries!" was the reply. I noticed that Jacob, the youngest, who was only 12 years old, was distracted during the Rosary. The religious sister who was next to him was slapping him gently and coaxing him to concentrate on the prayers. Then, as soon as the Rosary finished, the children stood up together and headed out to the sanctuary and towards the sacristy on the other side. My friend said, "Let's follow them. They are going to the apparition room". So we followed them across the sanctuary into the other sacristy, which was already packed with priests. In those days, a priest was never turned away. My friend and I squeezed in. The children were facing a blank wall, and began praying a Hail Mary in Croatian. Without any obvious cue, they dropped to their knees in perfect unison, and were caught up in a gaze beyond themselves. I noticed Jacob. No longer was he distracted. He was totally absorbed in something beyond himself. He was caught up in a vision and dialogue, which captivated him totally. I was convinced.

This could not be play- acted. However, I was scandalised by some Italian priests who had flash cameras and were flashing them right up against the visionaries' faces. Yet this again was for me a sign of authenticity. The children's poise was not disturbed at all. They didn't even blink when the flashes occurred before their faces.

I have always thought that Medjugorje and the Charismatic Renewal have an affinity built in heaven. While I have not seen it documented, I was told by Sr Briege McKenna, who for years has been engaged in a world-wide healing ministry, that when a group of leaders of the Renewal gathered in Rome to pray over Fr Jozo, who was later to become the parish priest of Medjugorje, she had a vision of a church with two white steeples and a sense that he was to be instrumental in aiding a new mission of the Blessed Virgin. This was a couple of years before the apparitions began. The spirit of Medjugorje, especially in its early days, was akin to that of the Renewal. Many people who were touched through Mary's presence in Medjugorje would be filled with the Holy Spirit and seek out prayer meetings or communities of the Renewal. Also many who had come to experience the new outpouring of the Spirit through the Renewal were led to go to Medjugorje to deepen in their love for our heavenly mother.

What has also convinced me about the supernatural activity at Medjugorje is the number of remarkable conversion stories that have occurred over the years since it began. When I was a regular visitor in the 80s and 90s it was such a privilege to sit in the confessional and listen to the Spirit moving in the hearts of those whose souls were open. In addition, countless young men and women have experienced a vocation to priesthood or consecrated life through Medjugorje. Possibly, over the years the tensions between the Franciscans and the local bishop have not been edifying. I trust the Vatican will soon be able to resolve matters in regard to the pastoral care of the pilgrimages, and indeed the on-going pastoral care of the visionaries. Whether what has been happening in recent years has muddied the waters I am not sure, but I am very sure that its origins are supernatural, and the Blessed Virgin Mary, Queen of Peace, did visit these children with prophetic messages for the world today.

From Darkness to Light

Michael Lightner grew up in a traditional Catholic family in Oconto, Wisconsin.[68] Nightly rosary and Mass on Sunday were non-negotiable. His Mum brought him a brown scapular home from Medjugorje. He only decided to wear it when he saw a fellow football player who he admired wearing one. High school football and athletics dominated his life. In college he quickly tossed his faith, pushed his Catholic upbringing aside, set his heart on football and women, both of which ended up disappointing him. To drown his sorrows he partied hard at the weekends, got into alcohol, experimented with drugs, which after a while began to control him.

Due to his hefty build, he became a bouncer and worked with security companies. Football was now coming good and he was in college first division and on his way to the National Football League. But then his mother found out about the drug dependency. She had one solution: "You are coming to Medjugorje". To placate his Mum he agreed to go. Walking alone down a lane in Medjugorje Michael made his first real prayer: "God, if you exist, I do not know you. I have never seen you or heard you. I've never felt you or had an experience of you. You could be the biggest con that twelve drunk men ever started 2,000 years ago. You've got seven days to prove yourself to me, otherwise I'm living my life the way I want to".

He had made a promise to his Mum that he would go to confession. So he lined up for English speaking confessions. Something happened in that cubicle. He couldn't see the priest behind the screen, but he just poured out everything for thirty-five minutes; every grisly detail of his sinful past – drugs, alcohol, beating people up, womanizing, stealing, lying. He was surprised the priest was not shocked. Michael was the one shocked. The priest gave some simple advice and a penance of five Our Fathers. It didn't seem enough. The priest said to meditate on one of the five wounds of Jesus during each Our Father. As the priest was declaring the words of absolution, Michael became aware of a physical presence within the confessional. His body from the knees up was pushed backward to a 30-degree angle, knocking his head on the back wall of the confessional. He couldn't sit up or move his body in any direction, not even an inch. With the words "I absolve you…" he felt an intense pain in his heart, as if a spear was plunged into his chest. He screamed in agony as he felt the spear being yanked out, and with it, his sins. "O my God," he said to himself, "He is real".

It took Michael forty five minutes to say five "Our Fathers" as he wept on his knees before a large Cross, watching a puddle of tears form on the ground. Pictures of people he had hurt flashed through his mind. For the first time he felt truly sorry. It was the hardest penance he had ever done. He made his way back into the Church and in his own words he said:

> At that very moment, God gave me a mystical experience. I received an anointing so sublime that it was better than any drug, better than any sex, better than winning the big game. All of those feelings combined could be multiplied by a million and not touch what God was doing in my heart. I felt as though I was levitating and was afraid to open my eyes because I literally believed I was on the ceiling. It was my Pentecost. God's Spirit, with its divine gifts and blessings entered my heart.

On a second visit to Medjugorje, the following year Michael visited the church close to the village where Fr Jozo was ministering. Pilgrims from many countries came to the church daily for healing prayer. Fr Jozo prayed first an impartation of the Holy Spirit over the priests present, and then they helped him pray over the rest of the people. Many people would rest in the Spirit when hands were laid upon them, a healing touch which often occurs in charismatic renewal. Michael volunteered to catch those who may fall down. He followed a Capuchin priest who was blessing people and almost all would fall. The priest came to a woman in a wheel chair, and kneeling before her in faith began to bless her head, shoulders, hips, thighs, knees, calves, ankles. Michael had time to engage in conversation with her husband. Apparently, his wife had a car accident seven years previously, and her spinal cord separated into two pieces. Then she later got spinal meningitis, which deteriorated her spinal cord below. For seven years, she had not moved a muscle beneath her waist.

Michael felt the Lord tugging at his heart. He wanted to go off and do other things. But the Lord was focussing him on this woman. He blurted out to the Lord, "Well, do you want me to pray for her? This one is impossible". He heard the Lord say, "Michael, if I get this woman up and make her walk will you enter the seminary?" "Absolutely not" was the answer. Michael squirmed for twenty minutes. How can I give up my football dreams? That has been the goal of my life! Yet he knew it was the Lord. He agreed to the deal. "Okay, Lord, get her up and walk her around this entire church, and I will enter the seminary". In five seconds, she was up on her feet without anyone telling her to do so. She went for a lap around the church! It took time for Michael to come through with the deal but in 2005, he was ordained a priest by Archbishop Timothy Dolan (now Cardinal).

The Gift of a Name

When the Missionaries of God's Love first began, we did not have a name. We simply called ourselves "The Fraternity" of the Disciples of Jesus Community. When Sr Briege McKenna was visiting Canberra in 1986, I asked her and Fr Kevin Scallon who was travelling with her, to pray over us. She was delighted to do so. They prayed with us for over an hour and delivered some bone thrilling prophecies. One of them was to ask Our Lady for a name. We did this and soon after the name came while I was praying in the chapel at the Redemptorist Monastery in Galong – Missionaries of God's Love. A couple of years later, when I was visiting Medjugorje, I was with a group of pilgrims who met with Mirjana. In those days, she used to experience Mary coming to her once a month and sharing intercessory prayer for the world with her. Someone asked Mirjana how Mary prayed. She answered, "It is different to what you would first think. She does not pray for heretics, or infidels, or pagans, or reprobates. Rather, she simply prays 'for those who do not yet know the love of God'". Mary is the first missionary of God's Love! That was confirmation for me of the name given by Mary. We are to go to those who do not yet know the love of God! And isn't this the mission of the whole Church?

10

MARY AS CHARISMATIC

A charism is "the manifestation of the Spirit for the common good" (1Cor 2:7). In other words it is a supernatural gift, empowering someone to do what otherwise would be impossible naturally. It is a gift for the sake of the church, which is given to build up the Church and aid in its mission to the nations.

Mary is the first charismatic. The Scriptural witness of Mary gives little indication of her being directly involved in marvellous actions or sensational events. Yet no other human being, apart from her Son, was so filled with the Holy Spirit. God used her to produce the greatest of all wonders, the birth of the Messiah. This happened because she had received power from on high, which came upon her with such effectiveness a child was conceived, who was the Son of God. This happened by the grace and power of the Spirit of God, Creator and Giver of life. While her fundamental charism is being Mother of Jesus, and hence Mother of all disciples, we can still find ample evidence in Scripture that she actually exercised charismatic gifts while on her earthly journey. There is no doubt she continues to do so through her ongoing glorious presence in the Church.

As the Mother of God, Mary is the most sublime example of a Spirit-filled person. She is the perfect recipient of the manifestation of God's power. But she is more than just an instrument of the Holy Spirit. That would be a far too impersonal and functional way of seeing things. She experienced the outpouring of the Holy Spirit in a *personal* way. In the upper room at Pentecost with the apostles and others, she received what the Church fathers called a "sober intoxication" of the Holy Spirit.[69] Yet there is no record of her engaging in the explosive apostolic preaching, healing and deliverance ministry that ensued from Pentecost. Her role was over and above that type of charismatic manifestation. She possesses and exercises the charism of Mother of the Church. This is the greatest charism of all the charisms given for the Church's mission. She exercises this charism constantly and generously without reserve. In doing so she reflects fully the mercy of God.

According to the New Testament the Church is founded on "the apostles and prophets". The "apostles" speaks of the Pope and the bishops, the institutional dimension. The "prophets" speaks of the charismatic dimension of the Church. Both dimensions are foundational to the Church and essential for the ongoing life of the Church. To lose one of these dimensions would be to diminish who we are as the people of God. In these times, we are witnessing a resurgence of the charismatic dimension, which had to some degree gone underground in centuries previous to the Second Vatican Council. Before the Council, many had thought the charisms had been given only to the Church in apostolic times to provide energetic impetus to the beginnings, but now they were no longer needed. In *Lumen Gentium*, the flagship document of Vatican II the matter was settled once and for all:

> It is not only through the sacraments and the ministrations of the Church that the Holy Spirit makes holy the people, leads them and enriches them with his virtues. Allotting his gifts according as he wills (cf. 1Cor 12:11), he also distributes special graces among the faithful of every rank. By these gifts he makes them fit and ready to undertake various tasks and offices for the renewal of the Church and building up of the Church, as it is written, "the manifestation of the Spirit is given to everyone for profit" (1 Cor 12:7).[70]

Pope John Paul II clarified this issue when in 1998, the year of the

Holy Spirit, he cried out passionately to thousands gathered in St Peter's Square:

> Open yourselves docilely to the gifts of the Spirit! Accept gratefully the charisms which the Spirit never ceases to bestow on us.[71]

He went on to assert strongly that the Church is essentially both institutional and charismatic; it would be erroneous to opt for one dimension over the other. The new surge of the Holy Spirit in our time has reawakened the use of the charisms amongst all the baptised. Whereas in previous centuries the proliferation of charisms in the early Church had been reduced to manifestations amongst the recognised saints, in our day they are once again being widely distributed and received gratefully by all who seek them.

Cardinal Suenens from Belgium, who had a key role as one of the four moderators of Vatican II, was largely responsible for the Council affirming the importance of charisms for the Church today. Prior to experiencing the Baptism in the Spirit he had been a strong supporter of the Legion of Mary, which at that time was sweeping the world. When he experienced a new awakening to the Spirit, he became a strong proponent of the link between Mary and the Holy Spirit. He was convinced that "Marian devotion will come to life in the proportion that it is linked to the Holy Spirit and lived under his guidance".[72] He also maintained, "to be receptive to the spiritual motherhood of Mary is an unfailing sign of our openness to the Holy Spirit".[73]

Mary is deeply connected with this charismatic renewal. We speak about the so-called "Marian" dimension of the Church being primarily about receptivity to the Holy Spirit, while the "Petrine" dimension is more about the institutional and hierarchical aspects of the Church. These are not in opposition with one another, but profoundly complementary and mutually supportive. Mary as Mother of the Church is at the heart of the charismatic dimension. It is no accident she was at Pentecost, when, in Luke's vision, the charismatic Church was birthed. She is always at the centre of God's innovative activity as the Spirit moves in new ways in the life of the Church.

The Charism of Intercession

In the Acts of the Apostles after Pentecost, we don't find Mary doing marvellous healings and preaching for conversion. I tend to think she probably stayed behind with others in the Upper Room interceding for the mission. The Church was expanding quickly under the new outpouring of the Spirit. We know little of her mode of presence within the Church at that time, but it must have been significant. We can suppose John's gospel was influenced by his having Mary in his home at Ephesus. Maybe Luke's gospel also was influenced by Mary, since travelling with Paul, he more than likely had contact with the Mother of Jesus. We can be sure Mary was given to charismatic intercession for the Church until the end of her earthly journey.

But this intercessory activity only came to its fulfilment when she was assumed into heaven. She had already been given to us definitively by Jesus as our mother. Now in heaven she could exercise her charism of motherhood most powerfully and universally. Just as she was used in God's plan to bring forth Christ through the power of the Holy Spirit, now by her intercession through the Church, Christ is being born in the hearts of many.[74] As Church, we are still, as at the beginning, "devoted to prayer together with Mary, the mother of Jesus", so that through her intercession our missionary efforts will advance the kingdom of God on earth.[75]

The gift of intercession is exercised in a totally unselfish way, pouring oneself out for the sake of others. Intercessors stand between God and his people. They allow God to work through them for the sake of others. They seek to jam the wavelengths of the devil, breaking any power the Evil One seeks to exercise by the authority of God. They are co-workers for the redemption of the world. Jesus is the one true Mediator in heaven "forever interceding for us" (Rom 8:34; Heb 7:25; Heb 4:16). All of our intercession is attained through him.

As we have seen in the previous chapter, we have one member of the Church who is magnificent in intercession: Mary, our Mother, now glorified. She is the most powerful intercessor. Due to her intimacy with her Son, her prayer is always in him, and hence always effective. So we confidently go to her to pray for us, and all the needs in the Church and the world. The earliest Marian prayer, the *Sub Tuum Praesidium*, is our constant refrain: "We fly to your patronage, O holy Mother of God. Despise not our prayers in our necessities, but ever deliver us from all dangers, O glorious and Blessed Ever Virgin."

When intercessors gather in a group to pray for the needs of others they invite the Blessed Virgin Mary to pray with them, just as she did at Pentecost. They open themselves to the movement of the Holy Spirit, waiting to gain a sense of what the Spirit is doing. They seek to get in touch with the burdens on the heart of God, and want to cooperate with his plan and offer themselves to accomplish this through prayer. With the Blessed Virgin Mary, Mother of the Church, they can gain insight quickly because she is living totally in the heart of God. We note before Pentecost how they prayed "in one accord" (Acts 1:14). If we intercede in union with Mary and the mind of the Church, much can be attained quickly.

Gift of Virginity

Another charism of the Blessed Virgin Mary is her virginity! The Church has always recognised virginity for the sake of kingdom as a supernatural gift bestowed on those consecrated to God. This grace enables them to do what otherwise would be impossible. Mary is uniquely both mother and virgin. She was a virgin before the Annunciation, but since she was betrothed to Joseph, it seems she had not chosen virginity as a way of life. It was only with the amazing grace of the Spirit coming upon her and the calling she received to be the mother of the Messiah that she knew she was called to remain virgin. Likewise, Joseph experiencing a profound calling to be the foster father of the Messiah knew implicitly that to take Mary to his home meant not only to become guardian of the family, but also to remain virgin. This reality in no way declares sexual intercourse in marriage to be negative or lacking in beauty and integrity. Virginity is simply an expression of a life given totally to God for the sake of the kingdom. Jesus himself deliberately remained virgin. It was a way of expressing the "existential urgency" of the kingdom of God and the need to have an "undivided heart" focussing all of one's energies for love and life upon God alone.

As a charism in the Church celibacy is very generative, birthing many in the faith and forming them in a life of discipleship. When it is a genuine calling and the gift is received whole-heartedly, the celibate has many spiritual children. Paul writes to his community in Thessalonika, "Like a mother feeding and looking after her own children, we felt so devoted and protective towards you, and had come to love you so much, that we were eager to hand over to you not only the Good News but our whole lives as well" (1Thess 2:7). Later when he was upset with the Galatians he chides them, "Must I go through the pain of giving birth to you all over again, until Christ is formed in you?" (Gal 4:19)

Those who are called to be consecrated to God in evangelical virginity will inevitably be drawn to the heart of Mary, as Virgin and Mother. Whether male or female, consecrated persons share in her virginal love for God, totally given to him and for his Kingdom. They also share in her motherhood as they birth many in the life of faith and discipleship in the Spirit. Mary is at the heart of that ecclesial activity of birthing others in the Spirit and nourishing them in the life of faith.

Gift of Praise

Mary has the manifest gift of exultant praise, which arises from the indwelling of the Holy Spirit. We see this sort of praise in the heart of Jesus, when the apostles shared the wonders they experienced on their first missionary outreach. Luke relates, "Filled with joy by the Holy Spirit he said, "I bless you Father, Lord of heaven and earth, for hiding these things from the learned and the clever and revealing them to mere children" (Lk 10:21). From the Greek text, the joy in the heart of Jesus was not just a pleasant feeling but rather an ecstatic outburst of jubilant praise. In Mary, the same exultant joy bursts forth after meeting Elizabeth and hearing Elizabeth relate how the child leapt in her womb:

> My soul glorifies the Lord and my spirit rejoices in God my Saviour. For he has looked on the lowliness of his servant. Yes, from this day forward all generations will call me blessed for the Almighty has done great things for me. Holy is his name! (Lk 1:46-49)

When we praise God in this way, the focus is not at all on ourselves but on the goodness, mercy, kindness, and all-powerful grandeur of God. Mary was caught up in the wonder of God's ways, which she had experienced personally. This praise usually starts with a spirit of gratitude, counting our many blessings. Then, as the heart expands by the Spirit's action, we cannot help but give God the glory and be captivated by the wonder of who he is. If the praise is sustained it leads to adoration, a deep heart-felt surrender to Almighty God with a simple acclamation such as "My Lord and my God".

Mary's Magnificat was modelled on the wonderful outburst of

praise, which Hannah had expressed after God had saved her from the embarrassment and shame of being barren. The new life in her womb, which had come to Hannah from the miracle of God's intervention, in response to her heart-felt cries, made her so overwhelmingly grateful that she just had to shout his praises. She rejoiced in God's saving power. Similarly, with the Blessed Virgin Mary, nothing could stop her from letting loose and praising God.

We have the prayer now in a stylised form. No doubt Luke captured the basic content. But we must ask the Spirit to put us in touch with Mary's heart at this moment. She was exploding with joy in the Spirit. She had known the mercy of God, his saving power, which she did not deserve. She was overwhelmed by his goodness. He had looked upon her in her "lowliness", or sometimes translated as her nothingness, or her poverty, or her humble state, radically dependent on God. Hence, all ages will call her blessed! Yes, she is so highly blessed because she is so aware of her nothingness, that everything she has is from God alone. It is all because he graciously looked upon her and raised her up. Thus her immense gratitude and joy. She can do nothing but exalt God for the great things he has done for her. And this awareness of being so favoured by God leads her through gratitude to sheer high praise, "Holy is his name! His Mercy is from age to age".

The account of Pentecost in Acts describes the Holy Spirit coming upon the assembly like tongues of fire, and they were all filled with the Spirit and began to speak in tongues and to prophesy. This is very inclusive language and we can presume the Blessed Mother experienced the same new effusion of the Spirit and enjoyed the manifestations that made people think they were drunk. At Pentecost Mary was right at the heart of the action. Undoubtedly, she is the first charismatic. She surely would have been lifted in exultant praise with this gift of the Spirit upon her and the apostles. They had waited together in eager expectation for the promise of Jesus to be fulfilled.

Now with this dramatic coming of the Spirit in tongues of fire filling all who were present, Mary's heart must have exploded with great joy. Just as a mother rejoices over the birth of her child so the Blessed Mother would have rejoiced to see the rebirth and transformation in the apostles. How could she not have blessed the Lord again and again for his greatness and awesome power and love.

Because of Mary's charism of praise and worship, which she continues to exercise in the heart of the Church, we sing the Magnificat daily in the evening prayer of the Liturgy of the Hours. In fact she is at the heart of all the Church's liturgical worship. We join with all the angels and saints, and in a particular way with the Blessed Virgin Mary in worshipping at the throne of God as we exult the Father in and through Jesus, in unity of the Holy Spirit. She teaches us how to worship and adore the Father and she draws us into the mystery of her Son's offering to the Father helping us to yield to the movement of the Spirit, so we can worship not only with "lip service" but in "spirit and in truth".

The Gift of Prophecy

From Scripture we can glean Mary's prophetic gifting. She moves in a prophetic spirit. She is called the "queen of prophets" in the Litany of Loreto. Prophets speak as messengers from God. They proclaim words inspired by the Holy Spirit. Contrary to popular thinking, prophecy is not foretelling the future, but rather proclaiming what God is doing right now out of love for his people. In the broad sense of the word, Mary's whole life was a prophecy, proclaiming the greatness of God. She brought *the* Word of God to the world.

Mary's Magnificat has often been referred to as a prophetic mode of prayer. She begins by exalting God with the Greek word *Megalynei* (Magnify) which elsewhere in Acts is associated with tongues: "they spoke in tongues and magnified God" (Acts 10:46). Tongues and prophecy are also found when Paul laid hands on people in Ephesus, "the Holy Spirit came down on them, and they spoke in tongues and prophesied" (Acts 19:6). This association of the two gifts occurs at Pentecost also (Acts 2:16-18). In her beautiful prayer of praise, Mary gives a prophecy of the fulfilment of God's plan given to Abraham. She also pronounces God's perspective on history and the way it is meant to unfold, which was at odds with the expectation of many.

> He puts forth his arm in strength and scatters the proud hearted. He casts the mighty from their thrones and raises up the lowly. He fills the starving with good things and the rich he sends empty away. (Luke 1:51-53)

These words echo those of the ancient prophets standing for the poor and oppressed, those identified as the *"anawim"*, the poor ones of God, who have been neglected and overlooked. She stands as one of these, who become the "holy remnant" faithfully waiting the Messiah. But her words are not only in regard to Israel's past. They speak of the present state of affairs; and they still speak to us today. God's way of working in history is contrary to the way the world usually thinks. He raises up the lowly, the humble, the poor; he brings down the proud, the arrogant, and the rich. All of this is prophetic prayer, which we still draw upon for inspiration today.

Mary's prophetic presence was evident from the greeting she gave to Elizabeth. We are not told what the greeting was, but more than likely, it would have been the standard *"Shalom"*, a blessing of peace. Her words had a momentous reaction within Elizabeth, who was carrying in her womb the sixth month old John the Baptist. Elizabeth exclaims, "The moment your greeting reached my ears, the child in my womb leapt for joy" (Lk 1:43). In a mysterious way John, who was the precursor, recognises Jesus within the womb of Mary and is delighted, jumping for joy. But it was the word of Mary, which provoked the response.

Mary's presence with Elizabeth brings new energy and hope for the task ahead of her. Elizabeth is relieved of worry over her child, released from the burden of her responsibilities and suddenly becomes full of joy. Now that Mary has come to her, Elizabeth is also given the gift of prophecy. She is the first to proclaim that the Messiah has come, and that he is the Son of God: "Who am I that the mother of my Lord should come to me?" How did Elizabeth know that her young cousin, Mary, was to be the mother of the Lord? Wherever Mary is present, the gifts of the Spirit are manifest.

Mary's words to the waiters at Cana after an apparent refusal by Jesus also bear the marks of prophetic inspiration. She knew the mind of Jesus even though Jesus gave no indication he would perform a miracle. She was supremely confident he would do something, "Do whatever he tells you" (John 2:5)

This gift of prophecy can be released more in the life of the Church as the Holy Spirit moves upon us. Mary will be at the heart of this outpouring. Prophecy grows the more the Holy Spirit comes upon us and fills us. The more we are obedient to the word of the Lord, like the Blessed Virgin, the more we will be used by him to speak prophetically. Jesus said of his mother, and of all his true disciples, "Blessed rather those who hear the word of God and keep it" (Lk 11:28). As we become more prompt and ready to speak the word of God this gift will develop in us.

The many apparitions of the Blessed Virgin in recent centuries are all in the mode of prophecy. Characteristically they give revelations of the merciful heart of God and also warnings for us to repent and pursue lives of holiness. In this book, I have referred to some of them. At Guadalupe, Fatima, Lourdes, Medjugorje and so many other locations Mary's prophetic appearances have been transforming the lives of millions.

11

HEALING AND MIRACLES

Mary ministers healing to us. This is one of her primary charismatic gifts. A friend shared with me recently that he was deeply touched by the presence of the Blessed Virgin while on an eight-day silent retreat. He had been struggling with a wounding in his sexuality from earlier years. He had gained a fair degree of victory in the area but in reflective time on the retreat he felt the pain of the deep scar and had shared it with his director. That afternoon as he was walking in the bushland around the retreat centre he came upon a little stream and a shady area. Then he sensed the presence of the Blessed Virgin, a profoundly feminine presence, but very holy. He knew it was Mary. No words were spoken, but her presence brought comfort and healing to his masculinity. The heaviness of the memory lifted and the pain disappeared. He was now more at peace within himself and at home with his sexuality in a new and confident way.

Testimonies like this are not rare. But it is hard to find anything in the New Testament that testifies directly to Mary's healing gift. Nevertheless, there's no doubt that she ministers healing. At first, it may seem that is not possible since Mary is the perfectly healed one. She never knew the emotional and spiritual scarring of sin. Neither did Jesus, yet he shared in our suffering which brought us healing. He was "pierced through for our transgressions, crushed for our sins". It was by his wounds we were to be healed. How does Mary fit into this healing mission? Even though she was given the grace of being conceived without sin, and living without sin, she suffered immense pain due to the sins of this fallen world. In no way was she indifferent to human suffering. From the crib to the Cross, she shared the human struggle. Her heart was wounded with compassion, which took her to the Cross with Jesus. Now she shares Christ's Risen life, she is Mother of Mercy and tenderness. She ministers healing to us through her motherly presence and intercession.

Mother of Tenderness

The testimony of one woman who had suffered sexual abuse as a child at the hands of a distant cousin shows the healing touch of Mary.[76] Judy had a deep, seething rage towards men due to the wounds of the childhood abuse. The influence of a generation of angry feminists, and years of sexual promiscuity as a young adult were supposed to liberate her. But she was still enslaved. She had recently become a Catholic and had been praying to Jesus for a revelation about Mary. That night she distinctly heard a woman's voice gently speaking to her, "I will cleanse your family". She knew it was the Blessed Virgin Mary. She said, "It was as though Our Lady came to take me by the hand and bring me on a journey through her own heart, to befriend me and show me a new way to be a woman – a woman in her very own likeness".[77] Judy was aware that while she appeared calm and confident exteriorly her interior emotions were erupting. She was angry and overwhelmed most of the time.

Going to a Christian counsellor Judy quickly realised that she was full of self-loathing and "secretly felt damaged, tarnished, and unclean." She was in dire need of healing. As she encountered the love of God more really, she began to love herself more, and to place her trust in God unconditionally. However, it was when she made a deliberate entrustment prayer to Our Lady that she gained the grace to forgive men who had hurt her in life, and especially the man who had abused her. She was able to decide to forgive. The feelings then came to match the decision. All the anger and negative emotions disappeared. "It was as though a river of pent-up hurt was released from my heart all at once, matched by a river of tears". She became more aware of the "unfavourable, combative thoughts" she had entertained about men and began to renounce them. The grace of entrustment to Our Lady had softened her and made her more pliable in the hands of God. She was letting God have his way with her.

Healing of the Church

In these days the whole Church is experiencing trauma. The disclosures of sexual abuse of children and young people by clergy and religious has shaken us to the core. We all share in the wound. Through the pain that we suffer so deeply God is still at work. He wants to purify us and render us more humble as a people, trusting more profoundly upon his redeeming love. Like a child in distress we need the soothing, calming presence of our loving Mother. She can minister healing to our wound. We stand together at the foot of the Cross with our Blessed Mother. Without her we may find this agonising experience unbearable. But with her comforting and consoling presence we can support one another, and find solace for all who are suffering from this trauma. As in the story above, maybe abuse survivors will find new hope through the embrace of our Mother of tenderness, but so will all of us in this moment of temptation to despair. She will lead us out of darkness into the loving heart of Jesus, our redeemer.

Maybe we could spend time meditating on Mary at Calvary as she cradled to herself the tortured body of Jesus after he was lowered from the Cross. In a mysterious way she is our mother of tenderness in our hour of distress. She shows us how to be with one another as we share the pain of this overwhelming tragedy. She saves us from making inadequate responses to this excruciating experience of trauma. We can be tempted to deny, or to diminish its significance, or to withdraw in self-protection, or to find superficial escape in busyness. Mary shows us another way. Her heart is large enough to embrace the pain, but without despair. As Church in these times we are being taught by Mary to listen to one another's hurt, to face the truth of our collective failure, to embrace one another with tenderness, and to humbly walk with one another into a future full of hope. Mary's embrace of the broken body of Jesus ultimately led to resurrection joy, and so also for us. Owning our pain, sharing in our weakness, by God's grace we will ultimately experience his strength, and will become wounded healers for others.

Our Mother who Performs Miracles for Us

Our loving Mother in heaven delights in interceding with her Son to perform miracles. An extraordinary instrument for this purpose is the so-called "miraculous medal" given by Mary to Catherine Laboure.[78] Catherine was the daughter of a well-to-do farmer in France. As a young woman, she experienced dreams of an elderly priest beckoning her to care for the sick. Long after this, when she visited the Daughters of Charity in Paris, she was surprised to see a picture of her nocturnal visitor on the wall. It was Vincent de Paul, the founder of the Congregation. Catherine knew she had to join the sisters.

In April 1830, she entered the convent. In July of that year, she had a dreamlike encounter with Our Lady who promised her with a mission that would be difficult, but she would be given the strength to fulfil it. Then in November on the same year, while in silent prayer with the other sisters in the chapel she experienced Our Lady appearing to her and revealing to her the design of a medal that was to be cut and distributed to as many as possible. The image was of Mary dressed in white, with a blue mantle and a veil "the colour of the dawn". Glittering rays streamed from her hands, and Catherine heard a voice saying, "These rays are a symbol of the graces that Mary obtains for her people". Framing the picture were the words: "O Mary conceived without sin, pray for us who have recourse to you". Then Catherine saw the reverse side of the image. It showed a cross standing over the letter M, with the hearts of Jesus and Mary underneath. She was to make a medal of these pictures as a model. The voice promised her everyone who wears the medal and prays its words devoutly "will enjoy the special protection of the Mother of God".

Catherine's spiritual director was initially highly sceptical of the vision. It was two years before he was convinced. After gaining the permission of the Archbishop of Paris, the medals were produced. Almost immediately, reports began to arrive of miracles occurring as a result of the medals. Her spiritual director began to keep track of the healings and miracles that were occurring. There were reports of cures from leprosy, tuberculosis, paralysis, fractures, epilepsy and tumours. Many who had fallen away from the faith were returning to the Church as a result of Mary's intercession through the use of the medal. Some experienced conversion for the first time in their lives. Her spiritual director received eighty such reports in September 1834. Five months later the number had risen to two hundred and twenty. It began to be called the "miraculous medal". As for Catherine, she deliberately led the rest of her life in obscurity tending to the needs of elderly men, caring for their physical needs as well as bringing them the love and tenderness of God. It was only after her death that people realised she was the one who had received the "miraculous medal" from Our Lady.

Conversion on Death Row

One highly celebrated conversion through the miraculous medal was Claude Newman.[79] His story was originally told by his confessor, Fr O'Leary, the chaplain to Warren County jail in Mississippi, who we suspect, as a result of recent research, may have embellished the details. Nevertheless, the factual story as related here is still miraculous. Claude Newman, 20 years old, was an illiterate Afro-American who had been sentenced to death by electrocution for killing his grandmother's husband, Sid Cook, in 1942. Newman was on death row when he noticed a fellow prisoner, Ralph Harris, who was a lapsed Catholic wearing a medal around his neck. He asked what it was about. The other prisoner was a bit embarrassed about it. But he offered it to Claude who had no religion. For some reason Claude felt he should put it around his neck. Later he told Sr Benna of the Holy Spirit sisters that he wanted to learn more about the woman depicted on the medal.

Claude then began to get dreams that disturbed him. One of them seemed to be a woman who was inviting him to send for a Catholic priest. Even though he had no previous connection with the Church, Claude told Sr Benna that the medal gave him "the feeling that he just had to belong to the Church of the Miraculous Mother". At Newman's request, the prison governor summoned Fr Robert O'Leary SVD, the chaplain to the local Afro-American community, to visit Claude. Claude asked to be instructed in the Catholic faith. So Fr O'Leary taught Claude about the Catholic faith and helped him receive the sacraments of baptism, reconciliation and holy communion. In the words of Fr O'Leary, Newman "readily grasped Catholic teachings and understood them so well that one could not help but feel God and his Blessed Mother were his teachers".

In the days leading up to his execution, Claude told the priest, "Father, now I know that God loves me. I feel so happy and peaceful as never before. Oh, if only I could be executed tonight and go to God." But the governor granted Claude a two-week stay, pushing his final day to February 4, 1944. Claude said that this delay merely prolonged his agony. Still he spent the rest of his days being a witness of faith to the other prisoners. On the morning of Claude's execution, Fr O'Leary heard Claude pray,

"Please Lord, help the other condemned men here". Claude prayed especially for a prisoner named James Samuel Hughes who hated him. Months after Newman's death, Hughes faced execution in the same electric chair as him. Hughes had killed a sheriff's deputy who tried to arrest him for incest. Hughes had impregnated his daughter, Annabelle, and sexually abused his other daughter, Esther. He was described by the chaplain as "the filthiest, most immoral person I have ever come across. His hatred for God and everything spiritual defied description". Moments before his death, to the utter surprise of everyone, Hughes expressed faith in Christ. The newspaper following his execution said that he "looked calmly up at the few present and said in clear-cut tones, 'I'm not afraid to confess the Lord Jesus Christ here tonight before man. May He have mercy on my soul, in the name of the Father, the Son, and the Holy Ghost'".

God answered Claude's prayer by helping another condemned man in the moment of his death.

Miracles at Lourdes

In 1858, Bernadette Soubirous was 14 years old. She was undoubtedly one of the most pitiable children in the small village of Lourdes in France.[80] Stunted from a cholera attack, she suffered regular bouts of asthma that left her clinging to the bars of the one window in the hovel where her family lived. She often went hungry and never attended school. She only knew how to recite the Rosary, which she loved to do using the cheap beads, which were always in her pocket.

One day while gathering wood along a mountain stream, the Gave, she saw a lady moving towards her within a golden coloured cloud. The lady beckoned her to pray the Rosary. Then she disappeared. This was the first of 18 apparitions. Word spread about the apparitions and crowds began to gather. At the ninth apparition, people were shocked. Bernadette moving around on her knees suddenly bent low and began digging in the frozen ground with her fingers. Muddy water seeped into the hole she made. She scooped up the water in her hands, drank and smeared some over her face. They thought she had gone mad. But later Bernadette said, "She told me to drink and wash at the spring she indicated".

Most onlookers left in disgust. Some stayed on. Gradually a stream was developing. The flow kept increasing. A former quarry worker, Louis Bouriette, half-blind from an accident when a blast had taken out one of his eyes, had his daughter dip a cloth in the water. He prayed, touched his eye with the water, and his sight was restored. Now the crowds came in earnest. Our Lady's messages began to become a strong call to repentance before it is too late, the message of the gospel.

The parish priest, who was finding it difficult to believe the authenticity of the apparition, kept demanding Bernadette to ask the lady her name. Finally, the name was given, "I am the Immaculate Conception". Bernadette had no idea what that meant. Her catechism classes had been negligible. The dogma of the Immaculate Conception had only been officially defined by the Pope four years previously. But Bernadette had her answer, given in her own dialect. So she ran to the priest's house repeating the name over and over. Bursting into the house she blurted out, "I am the Immaculate Conception!" For a moment, the startled priest thought she must have gone mad. But then he realised there was no way Bernadette would have known those words. He was convinced. He would build the little shrine that the Lady had been requesting. And the rest is history. Millions of people flood to Lourdes annually. Countless miracles of healing have been recorded.

Healing of Multiple Sclerosis

One such miracle was Peader Clarke.[81] As a young man growing up in Ireland, he loved sport – football, hurling and athletics. But occasionally his body would give way suddenly. He would lose power in his legs and become dizzy. The doctor put it down to vertigo. After marrying Terry he would get frustrated sometimes when driving. His foot would have a spasm and slip from the pedal. It came to a peak one day when he couldn't judge the distance between cars, bumping into them, and feeling really weird as he got out of the car.

A medical examination came up with the explanation – multiple sclerosis. That was in 1988 and he spent a whole year in hospital getting worse and worse. His speech became slurred and jumbled, and he had bad memory lapses. He couldn't get out of bed by himself and he was incontinent.

Terry had to work by serving drinks in a local club. When the members found out about Peader they got together and collected money for the couple to go to Lourdes. Terry explained the offer to Peader in one of his more lucid moments. He agreed since "I already have one foot in the grave". They took the plane to Lourdes. He was unconscious all the way. He recalls becoming conscious as he looked at the statue of the crowned Virgin in the large Esplanade. "Gazing at her face," he said, "I lost all my fear of death. Dying was going home to God and a great peace swept over me. Ah, I thought, this is my Lourdes miracle".

On the last day of the visit, he remembers hearing part of a homily in which the priest was saying, "love is not love until you give it away". He says he began doing that. He could see how much Terry and her mother were crying that he begged Our Lady to fix that. He managed to roll out of his wheel chair at the very spot where the spring first began. He noticed how his wife and mother-in-law were still crying. He complained to Mary, "You are not listening to my prayers. They are still crying".

Getting back to his room, he was keen to dismiss his wife because he really felt this was when he was going to die. He said,

> I closed my eyes waiting for merciful death when one of those spasms hit me, ending me up on the floor. Another spasm twisted my head and I found myself looking directly at the Crucifix on the wall. I got a fright at first because I could see it despite there was no light. Then I said as a kind of prayer to Him: "Let's give it one more go at staying alive". Suddenly I saw a most beautiful woman standing by the crucifix. I cannot describe the beauty except to call it total sinlessness. That may not make sense to anyone else but…Anyhow she smiled at me and I felt sure it was the Mother of Jesus.

Peader began to think he must be hallucinating from all the drugs they had been giving him. He rubbed his eyes. She was still there. She was now with Bernadette in front of the grotto. There were many people there in great physical distress. He was convicted to pray for them. Then he noticed that Our Lady was looking at the crucifix and then turned back to him. She seemed to be saying: "Look at my suffering".

Then Peader realised he was standing and that he could walk. He could use his toes and his feet. He just walked down to his wife's room. She was overwhelmed and couldn't speak. They just knelt down there and then to pray the Rosary. He could not only walk, he could run, which he promptly did to the amusement of all, up and down the stairs effortlessly.

Peader and his wife had never been blessed with children, but now the Lord had given them a ministry. They spent the next years of their life organizing for others who were seriously ill to get to Lourdes. Not all are healed, but all who go to Lourdes with an open heart experience the tender mercy of the heart of our God, ministered to them by our loving Mother.

12

MOTHER OF EVANGELISATION

Mary joined the disciples in praying for the coming of the Holy Spirit at Pentecost. This made possible the extraordinary outburst of missionary activity which birthed the Church. She continues to pray at the heart of the Church for conversion of all to be reborn in the Spirit. Wherever Mary is there is the Holy Spirit, and wherever the Holy Spirit is Mary's presence is no surprise. She is woman of the Spirit. As Mother of the Church, she continues to birth sons and daughters in the Spirit.

The Beloved Disciple, standing at the foot of the Cross, representing all disciples heard Jesus direct him to Mary as his mother, "Behold your mother!" This was a prophetic command. Jesus did not want us to journey without a mother. Whenever there is something lacking in our mission she is there, bringing it to the attention of her Son, "they have no wine". She encourages us to "do whatever he tells you". When we experience tribulations in mission and endure rejection and ridicule, she is with us as a sign of hope. Having been pierced through suffering at the foot of the Cross she understands our pain as we share in the saving mission of her Son, and she draws near to us and opens our hearts to her motherly love. With Mary, we find the revolutionary nature of love and tenderness, which is meant to characterise all of our evangelising activity. These qualities make us strong, because we do not need to treat others poorly in order to feel important about ourselves. The way of mercy and compassion is God's way and she shows us this way.

Mary was indeed the first evangelist. After hearing from the angel that in God's unfathomable plan she was to be the mother of the Messiah, and having made her unconditional response to this invitation, she did not retire into self-enclosed seclusion. The angel had told her that Elizabeth her cousin, who was past childbearing age and had never been pregnant, was now in her sixth month. This was a sign to Mary that "nothing is impossible to God". Rather than stay in the comfort of her own house, Mary immediately went "with haste" to visit Elizabeth. The sense of the language here is that she went as quickly as she could. It was not an easy journey. Probably undertaken by foot over the Judean hills, the journey would have lasted many days and held dangers on the road. But this strong woman of God was not deterred by obstacles. Her heart was full of compassion for her cousin who would need assistance in the latter months of pregnancy and during the child's birth. Here we have a clear example of other-centred care with a heart of self-sacrificing service.

When Mary arrived at Zechariah's house, she went inside to greet Elizabeth. Her presence was spiritually electrifying. We remember the words of Pope Paul VI: "The Holy Spirit is the principal agent of evangelisation".[82] With Mary's greeting, Elizabeth was immediately filled with the Holy Spirit. Encountering her Spirit-filled cousin, Elizabeth experienced the overflowing love and power of God come upon her. The Holy Spirit within Mary was imparted to Elizabeth who in that moment was baptised in the Spirit. The Spirit of joy in Mary's heart was infectious. Elizabeth was filled with joy, and the child in her womb leapt for joy as he recognised the Saviour. "Why should I be honoured with a visit from the mother of my Lord? For the moment your greeting reached my ears, the child in my womb leapt for joy".

Mary is a model of how we are to evangelise as Church. Her joyful presence in the Spirit and the words she speaks were contagious. The joy was irresistible. When we evangelise, what is most important is not so much our arguments or explanations, but rather the joyful proclamation of the Christ who lives within us. Mary shows us how to bear Christ to the world. Her presence and her words convey the joy she knows from the Love within her womb. We are also bearers of the good news of Jesus whom we have met personally and know intimately. This witness is highly attractive to any human heart.

The deepest questions of every human heart can only be answered by Jesus. The deepest longing of each person can only be ultimately satisfied by Jesus. The leaping of John the Baptist in the womb of Elizabeth is a promise of the quickening in the hearts of our contemporaries as we give witness to the joy and hope that is within us. The faith we have in the risen Christ, whom we know personally, is spiritually electric in its impact on others. With Mary we allow our presence of joy in Christ to touch the hearts of others by the work of the Holy Spirit and awaken them to what they had not known before – that the lasting treasure for every heart is Jesus, Christ, the Lord.

Mary is our mother in evangelising. If we take Pope Francis' image of the Church as a field hospital in the midst of a battle, then Mary is with us, ever tender-hearted, inspiring us to pick up the wounded and care for their needs. Our evangelising will always have a strong dimension of healing. So many have been damaged by relational breakdowns, anxiety or depression, loss of meaning and purpose, disappointments and rejection. Mary is there drawing them to Jesus and letting the Holy Spirit give them new hope and direction in life.

But we must remember the heart of the work of evangelisation is personal prayer. Mary again is our example. She is the one who "keeps all these things, pondering them in her heart" (Lk 2:19). She is always in touch with the movement of the Holy Spirit in daily life and in the Church and the world. It is important to be with Jesus first, and then he sends us out on mission. To be "stewards of the mystery of Christ" we must first be captured by the fire of his love. Like the man in the gospel parable, when we find the treasure, which is God's love, we are filled with such joy that we will do anything to possess this treasure and to share it with others. To enter deeply into this mystery we need time aside in silence and solitude. Great words arise out of silence and return to silence. Hours of silent prayer in solitude, or before Jesus in the Blessed Sacrament, provide the authentic grounding for evangelisation. This is the highest priority. In the quiet, we give him permission to penetrate the heart with love and slowly we become more like him, and can authentically proclaim who is.

A Mother's Missionary Heart

An extraordinary example of Mary's missionary heart is the way she was central to the evangelisation of Latin America. The appearance of Our Lady of Guadalupe to Juan Diego, a humble Aztec Indian generated the conversion of Mexico and, indeed, the whole of Central America.[83] In the 16th Century the Aztec empire ruled from the Gulf of Mexico to the Pacific Ocean, including Mexico, Guatamala, Belize, and portions of Honduras and El Salvador. Montezuma, seen as the earthly representative of the sun god, was King of the Aztecs and ruled from an island in Lake Texcoco, the site of modern Mexico City. This capital city was the centre of religious worship for the Aztecs, who believed the sun struggled at night as it confronted mortal enemies living in the dark underworld, and then rose triumphant every morning. But the victory was short-lived. Any night according to this cosmology could be the last night. The Aztecs lived in mortal fear that the coming night could be the end. To help the sun in the battle, they believed the gods needed human blood to subsist. To appease this insatiable thirst of the gods the priests sacrificed thousands of human lives every year. One hope they had was that the Mother of the Sun god, a deity called Tonantzin would appear to save the Aztec nation and the world.

When the Spanish Conquistadors arrived, they conquered the Aztecs, destroyed Temples, and tried to abolish the ancient religion. But they found great resistance to Christianity. The Christian missionaries who came with the colonisers were making little headway in bringing the faith to the Mexican people. While human sacrifices were banned, the new rulers were often cruel and ruthless in their treatment of the indigenous people often reducing them to slavery and branding them like cattle to be sold at will. Many of the Franciscan, Dominican and Augustinian missionaries laboured tirelessly to build schools, hospitals and communicate the faith to the locals. But the indigenous people were understandably highly resistant to the religion of the Conquistadors, who had killed thousands of Indians, raped their women and destroyed their capital city. However, a newly appointed bishop Zumarraga, a Franciscan, who was sympathetic to the plight of the Indians, was working hard to relieve their dire oppressive situation. He was aware that the Indians were close to insurrection and their sheer numbers could mean the Spanish colonisers would be annihilated.

Into this highly emotionally charged situation, the Blessed Mother intervened. She appeared to Juan Diego, a child-like, simple peasant widower at the age of 55. He had already become a practising Catholic, regularly attending Mass and catechism classes. At daybreak, on Saturday 9 December 1531, Juan Diego was on his way to Church. As he passed a hill named Tepeyac, on which previously stood a temple to the fearful Aztec Mother of the Sun god Tonantzin, he heard songbirds burst into harmony. For the Aztecs this was a sign of something divine about to happen. A beautiful woman appeared to him, bathed in golden beams of the sun. She called him by name in Nahuatl, his native language, "Juan Diego!" She told him that she loved him as her "dear little son" and that she was the "Virgin Mary, Mother of the one true God, of Him who gives life". She requested a temple be built in that place. She disclosed herself as full of mercy for all. She promised to take those who are weeping and sorrowful to her heart, and to cure their sufferings and afflictions. She told Juan Diego to run to tell the bishop.

Juan Diego arrived at the bishop's palace to be treated with contempt by the servants. He was finally granted an audience with the bishop who was cordial but obviously sceptical about the request. Juan returned to the hill and found Mary waiting for him. He begged her to send someone more suitable to deliver her message "for I am a nobody". The beautiful woman sent him back to the bishop to "repeat to him my great desire for a church in this place". So, Sunday morning, 10 December, Juan Diego, after much difficulty from the bishop's staff was granted another audience with the bishop, who was surprised to see him. The bishop instructed Juan to ask for a sign. Juan Diego dutifully reported this to the Virgin. She told him to return the following morning for the requested sign. However, when Juan returned home he found his uncle Juan Bernardino seriously ill. Instead of going back to Tepeyac, he stayed home with his dying Uncle.

Then early on Tuesday morning, 12 December, he left the house to find a priest for his uncle to receive the last rites. He had to pass by Tepeyac hill, but went a different route than before to avoid any apparition. But to his consternation she still appeared to him on that new route. The Virgin asked him what the problem was. He was embarrassed and apologised for not coming the day before because his uncle was dying. Then the Lady said the famous words, *"Am I not here, who am your Mother? Are you not under my shadow and protection? Am I not the fountain of your joy? Are you not in the fold of my mantle, in the cradle of my arms?"* She assured him his uncle's health had been restored. He could give up his errand and now do hers. She told him to go to the top of the hill and cut flowers growing there and bring them to her.

Juan Diego knew that flowers don't grow in December. But he obeyed. Surprised, he found beautiful Castilian roses on the hilltop. He had never seen flowers like this before. As he cut them, he cradled them in his tilma to protect them from the cold. A tilma is a long cloth cape worn by the Aztecs, and often used to carry things. He ran back to Mary and she rearranged the roses and tied the lower corners of the tilma behind his neck so nothing would spill. She told him this is the sign for the bishop. He was to keep it hidden in his tilma until he reached the bishop, and also to let the bishop know his uncle is healed. When Juan finally reached the bishop, after enduring the mockery of the servants, other advisers were present. Juan immediately opened the tilma and let the Castilian roses fall to the ground. He did not expect the shock on the bishop's face, who after seeing the roses, was now staring agape at Juan Diego's tilma. On the tilma was the perfect image of the Blessed Virgin as described by Juan. The bishop and his advisers were now kneeling on the floor before Juan Diego. There was no doubt anymore. The roses could not have grown naturally; they were only known in Spain. The image on the tilma was clearly a miracle. The Virgin Mother had intervened.

The impact of this apparition was enormous. News spread like wildfire! The indigenous people were attracted immediately. This was not an imposition upon them from a foreign ruling culture. This was something from within their own language and culture. The Virgin Mary had spoken in Nahuatl, the Aztec language, and appeared to an Indian, not to a Spaniard. She appeared at Tepeyac, the place all associated with Tonantzin, the Mother of the Sun god of the Aztecs. Mary was now presenting herself as the Mother of the true God, and the Christian faith was to replace that of the Aztecs. And the Indians who lived in a culture of symbols and pictures grasped quickly the meaning of the tilma. The true sacrifice that brings freedom is not shedding of blood to appease the anger of the Aztec gods, but the one sacrifice of Jesus, who shed his blood out of love to save us and give us new life. Over the next seven years, from 1531 to 1538, eight million indigenous Mexicans were converted to the Catholic faith.

The tilma carried all the imagery that spoke so powerfully to the local people. It signified Mary bringing her Son, Jesus Christ, to the new world through one of their own. She appears as a beautiful young Indian maiden, with a gaze of love and compassion. Her rose dress, adorned with a jasmine flower, eight petal flowers, and nine heart flowers were all symbols of the Aztec culture. Her blue mantle symbolised royalty and the blue itself symbolised life and unity. She appeared on the day of the winter solstice, with the rays of the sun behind her, indicating she is greater than the Sun god, which the Aztecs had worshipped. Instead of the uncertain promise of salvation from the Mother of the Sun god, they now had certain salvation proclaimed through the Mother of the resurrected Son of God. And most interestingly she wore a black maternity band, showing she was pregnant. The baby who Mary was carrying within her, the Word made flesh, is now the centre of the universe. She was wearing the Cross on the brooch around her neck indicating the Son of God who died on the Cross brought salvation to all humankind. Those who knew the Scriptures could easily identify her as the woman of Revelations: "A great sign appeared in the sky, a woman clothed with the sun, with the moon at her feet, and on her head a crown of twelve stars" (Rev 12:1).

This apparition of the Blessed Virgin in the Americas is undoubtedly one of the most amazingly effective missionary interventions in the history of the Church. The miracle of Guadalupe led to a huge wave of conversions. Her influence in the whole of Mexican history was enormous. The secret of her evangelising was that she appeared within the culture, not over and above the life of the people. She appeared to an Aztec, not to a European. She was dressed in local attire, spoke the local language, communicated through local signs, and symbolically expressed in their language the pre-eminence of Jesus over their local gods. Her mode of communication was gentle and tender-hearted in stark contrast to the ferocious and demanding Aztec gods. The image on the tilma according to scientific expectations should have faded by now, and has survived fire and earthquake, but seems indestructible. This was her way of leaving a lasting legacy that rationalists have found hard to dispute.

In more recent times in the Western world, she has become popular as the heavenly advocate for the child in the womb. In the contemporary "culture of death" where abortion has become widely accepted, she has become the sign of fertility and protection of life. Through her missionary image, Mary has melted the hearts of many women who have planned to have an abortion. Many stories can be told of Mary's intercession on behalf of the unborn. Only one can be told here.

One day in Wichita Kansas, when the image of Our Lady of Guadalupe was placed in a public park for veneration a pregnant mother named Vicki was walking by.[84] She had already decided to abort her baby. But the image caught her eye. She stopped, her knees were shaking and she began to cry. She later said that when she saw the missionary image "it was like the Holy Spirit was coming into me and waking me up after many years". Vicki did not know the significance of the image, but she heard a voice inside saying to her, "You are called to motherhood!" She right there and then decided not to go ahead with the abortion but to choose life and put her trust in God. She found people who could care for her through the pregnancy and eventually gave birth to a beautiful baby boy. Vicki returned to her Catholic faith and now spends her life helping mothers with their unborn children.

Our Lady of Kurduntiga

Australia has its own story of Our Lady initiating a mission amongst our indigenous people.[85] The first Catholic missionaries arrived at Port Keats (known locally as Wadeye) on Sunday 30 September 1934. There were seven feuding tribes torn apart by a never-ending round of 'pay-back' murders. The number of people left had been reduced to 160. Alarmed at the extent of the trouble, the government had requested Catholic missions to go there to establish peace. In taking up the challenge, Fr Richard Docherty MSC knew his life could be in danger. However, when he arrived he erected a picture of Our Lady with her foot on the serpent, the popular image of the time to represent her as the New Eve. Mary would fulfil the promise given by God after the fall that a woman would crush the head of Satan depicted as a serpent.

Unknown to Fr Richard the Blessed Virgin had gone before him. Ten years before his arrival a local man named Mullingin, while taking a rest in the afternoon, was dozing when "he was suddenly brought to life by the sound of wind that resembled the flapping wings of birds". He heard a voice say: "Close your eyes and I will take you to a good place". Afterwards the voice told him to open his eyes. He found himself in a dream-like vision of heavenly paradise in which an angel pointed out to him a beautiful woman. The angel told him, "That's our mother standing over there, the boss lady. She's treading on a snake". The snake was trying to get loose but "the great lady, the *Kardu Mutchinga*", would tread on it again.

When the people returned home from fishing that day, they found Mullingin a transformed man. Before this dream he had been given to violence and murder. People were afraid of him. But as soon as they arrived back at the camp Mullingin gathered them together saying, "Come here! We're going to sing and dance something new now". He sang for them the *Mulurn Kanarra* song. Then he told them all about the great woman, the *Kardu Mutchinga*. He told them how she was standing on some round thing with a snake under her feet. He said the voice kept telling him… "that is the woman!" The people were amazed at the new radiance in Mullingin's face and how gentle he now was, encouraging the people not to fight anymore.

Ten years after this vision, some of Mullingin's companions visited the newly established Catholic mission. They saw the picture of Mary with her foot crushing the serpent. Through an interpreter, they heard what Fr Docherty had to say about her. They immediately realised it must be the woman Mullingin had met in his vision. They quickly returned to the camp at Kurduntiga to inform him of what they had seen. Mullingin hastily returned with them to the mission. Without any hesitation he proclaimed, "Yes, that's the one. That's the one I saw in my dream".

The impact of this story of the way Our Lady had already come to the people through Mullingin's experience was powerful for the Wadeye tribes. A new unity came to the people as they embraced the Catholic faith and were able to integrate the different tribes into one community. The local council is called "Kardu Numida" proudly proclaiming their identity – "one people".

A Marian Way

A "Marian" way of evangelisation is the Church's way of proclaiming the good news. It arises out of deep heart-felt prayer, is motivated by love, with a heart of mercy and compassion for all who do not yet know the love of God. It reaches out to those on the peripheries, who have been overlooked or marginalised in the society. When a need is exposed, it acts with haste in the service of others. It is a Spirit-filled evangelisation, which proclaims the good news of Jesus with boldness, stirring a response of repentance and faith, and imparting the baptism in the Holy Spirit with fire. It meets people "where they are at", according to age, intelligence, psychological capacity and emotional stability. It uses the symbols of the culture, affirming all that is good in culture and challenging what needs transformation. It provides a way of discipleship in a life of virtue within a face-to-face community, and it prepares those who have evangelised to quickly become evangelisers.

ENTRUSTMENT TO MARY

I want to share with you the Missionaries of God's Love entrustment prayer. This is my humble gift to you. We feel there is an anointing of the Spirit on this prayer, which we pray daily. You will notice that I have avoided calling it a prayer of consecration. We "consecrate" ourselves to Jesus, not to Mary. We consecrate ourselves to the wounded heart of Jesus, broken open in love for the world. In the Catholic tradition, some have chosen to consecrate themselves "to Jesus through Mary"[86]. That's fine. But I prefer the language of entrusting myself to our loving Mother, who takes me to Jesus.

Immaculate Heart of Mary,
I entrust myself to you.
Draw me into the heart of Jesus, your Son.
Share with me the mystery of his Cross,
And the fire of his Spirit.

Gentle Mother,
Since Jesus gave me to you from the Cross,
I am yours.
Nurture me in his love,
And help me to pray.
Guide me in his Spirit,
And teach me his ways.

Pure and Chaste Virgin,
As I place my life in your hands,

Bring me closer to Jesus, your Son.
Make me obedient to the Father
And humble of heart.
Have eyes of mercy on me in my weakness,
Protect me from the evil one,
And bring healing grace to my life.
So with your spirit of gratitude and praise
I may have your heart for the mission
To spread the Good News of God's love,
Now and always. Amen.

The prayer is addressed to "Immaculate heart of Mary". Her Mother's heart is always for us. Her heart is totally pure, undefiled, given for us. Her heart is one with the heart of Jesus. She is the perfect way to his heart. We ask her: "Draw me into the heart of Jesus, your Son". All holiness is found in the heart of Jesus, which Mary is able to open up to us so readily. We want to know Jesus intimately, love him unconditionally, and serve him with our lives.

We ask her to share with us the mystery of his Cross and the fire of his Spirit. We want our hearts to burn with the fire of love in the heart of Jesus as he hung on the Cross for the sake of all men and women. She stood at the foot of the Cross. No one can take us into the mystery of his sacrificial love for humanity as she can. We want this fire of love to be in us also. The fire of love in Jesus was sustained by the Holy Spirit. He longed to bring this gift to all. "I have come to bring fire to the earth and how greatly I am constrained until it is accomplished" (Lk 12:49). At Pentecost this burning desire was fulfilled. The fire of love, the Spirit of God, was poured out in abundance "upon all flesh". Mary was there in the Upper Room. She can take us into this mystery and open up to us the wonderful gift of being "baptised by the Holy Spirit and fire", as Jesus promised.

I address her as "gentle Mother". The tender heart of our dear Mother is given for us. As he hung on the Cross, Jesus gave John the Beloved to her. "Behold your mother". He thus gave me to her as my Mother. Because of this I can confidently entrust myself to her with the words, "I am yours". I am not an orphan. Jesus promised the Spirit so we become a son or a daughter of God, able to call God, Abba, Father. In the Spirit, he also gave us a tender Mother, who ensures we receive all the graces and gifts of the Spirit we need. I entrust myself into her loving hands, knowing that she wants only for me to be filled with the Spirit so I become more like Jesus.

Just as Mary nurtured Jesus as he was growing in wisdom, age and grace, so with us. We ask her to "nurture me in his love, and help me to pray". She taught Jesus to pray when he was a child. She wants to teach us the word of God also. She will form in us a contemplative heart. We ask her to "guide me in his Spirit and teach me his ways". She who knows the heart of Jesus most fully is such a wise, firm guide and teacher. We ask her to form us in the beatitudes, which she lived so perfectly; the way of Jesus, the qualities of his heart that we need to be formed in us.

We place ourselves in the hands of the "pure and chaste Virgin". We desire to be pure of heart, and fruitful in virtue. A little later we pray, "Have eyes of mercy on me in my weakness. Protect me from the evil one. And bring healing grace to my life". The Blessed Virgin brings healing to those areas of our past life where there has been disorder and wounding. In our weakness, we know her eyes of mercy, which reflect perfectly the merciful heart of God. By God's grace, through her loving intercession, we are recreated and given new freedom for life.

We come to our Mother of mercy in all our needs. In our brokenness, her tender gaze upon us gives hope. She lets us know that God's heart is always turned towards us. As our dear Mother who is refuge of sinners, we run to her for help. When we fall, we gain new heart from her tender mercy. We obtain the grace to stand up again and persevere on the journey, looking not at our failure but at the merciful heart of God mediated through her gaze upon us. In the spiritual battle, she throws her mantle of protection over us.

At all times Mary brings us closer to Jesus, her Son. She shares the graces of her heart with us, making us humble before God and obedient to the will of the Father. With Mary at our side, we can be more fully surrendered to God's will and faithful in following Jesus as his chosen disciple. From her poverty of spirit, we can gain her "spirit of gratitude and praise". Her Magnificat becomes ours as we exalt the Father for his graciousness to us. We praise Jesus for his saving power, which we could not earn, and are full of gratitude for the recreating work of the Spirit, which is sheer gift to us. With Mary, we cannot stop praising the Lord even when we are in the midst of great adversity. We will praise him in all circumstances, because that is what she wants us to do.

Finally, we pray that we would have Mary's heart for the mission of spreading the good news of God's love to all whom we meet. We ask her to give us the grace to preach the good news of Jesus in season and out of season, and to make this our life's work in thoroughgoing service. She intercedes "for those who do not yet know the love of God"; the ones to whom we have been sent. With her heart of love, we go to the weak, the broken, the impoverished, bringing the hope and light of Christ. This is our purpose. This is the mission of the whole Church.

ENDNOTES

1. Pope Paul VI, *Marialis Cultus*, 29-38
2. ibid., 33
3. I wish to acknowledge that the first three chapters have been inspired by Raniero Cantalamessa, *Mary Mirror of the Church*, Collegeville Minnesota: The Liturgical Press, 1992,
4. Bernard of Clairvaux, *Homilies in Praise of the Virgin Mother*, 4,8-9
5. Irenaeus of Lyons, Adversus Haereses III, 22,4
6. Therese of Lisieux, *Story of a Soul*, (Washington: ICS, 1972) p.194
7. St John of the Cross, *Collected Works* (Washington: ICS,1972) pp 721-722
8. Pope Francis, Homily for Mass on Marian Day in the Year of Faith, October 13, 2013, St Peter's Square
9. Carlo Carretto, *Blessed are You Who Believed*, (London: Burns&Oates, 1982)pp.3-6
10. Pope John Paul II, *Redemptoris Mater*, 18
11. ibid.,18
12. Pope John Paul II, *Salvifici Doloris*, 22
13. ibid., 27
14. Judy Landrieu Klein, *Mary's Way*, (Notre Dame, Indiana, Ave Maria Press, 2016)
15. Teresa of Avila, *Interior Castle*, Collected Works Vol II, IV,1,7 (Washington DC: ICS publications, 1980)
16. Pope John Paul II, *Rosarium Virginis Mariae*, Apostolic Letter on Rosary, 18
17. Ibid., 24
18. Ibid.,43

19 The title "servant of God" is the first step towards canonisation. Eileen O'Connor's story and spirituality is outlined in Jocelyn Hedley, *And Here Begin the Work of Heaven*, Sydney: St Pauls Publications, 2011.
20 Ibid., p.89
21 This story is told in Jocelyn Hedley, op.cit., pp.90-92
22 Joseph Langford, MC, *Mother Teresa: In the Shadow of Our Lady*, (Huntingdon, Indiana: Our Sunday Visitor, 2007) 39
23 ibid., pp 74-75
24 ibid., p.42
25 ibid., p.43
26 Francis J. Moloney, *Mary Woman and Mother*, p.38
27 ibid., pp 46-47
28 Pope Francis, Homily for Solemnity of Mary Mother of God, Jan.1 2017, St Peter's
29 ibid.
30 ibid.
31 ibid.
32 ibid.
33 Pope Francis, Homily for Solemnity of Mary Mother of God, Jan 1, 2018, St Peter's
34 This phrase given in *Virgin Mary Appears to Mirjana* in Medjugorje, Youtube, July 2, 2019
35 Pope Francis, Catechesis on prayer for the Marian Year of Faith, Oct 12, 2013 St Peters Square
36 Irenaeus, Adversus Haereses III, 22,4
37 Pope Francis, Homily Solemnity of Mother of God, Jan 1st 2019, St Peter's Basilica
38 Lumen Gentium, 63
39 Pope John Paul II, Redemptoris Mater, 43-44

40 Pope Francis, Homily at Memorial Mass of Mary Mother of Church in Casa Santa Marta 21st May 2018
41 Ibid.
42 ibid.
43 Pope John Paul II, Letter to women, June 29, 1995 Vatican
44 Judy Landrieu Klein, *Mary's Way*, (Notre Dame, Ave Maria press, 2016) p.95
45 Bishop Thomas J. Olmsted, Into the Breach, Apostolic Exhortation to Catholic Men, Diocese of Phoenix, September 29, 2015
46 Pope John Paul II, Meditation with the Italian Bishops, from the Policlinico Gemelli, Insegnamenti, Vol XVII/1, 1994, p. 1061
47 The story is well known. A brief account can be found in Paul Glynn, *Healing Fire from Frozen Earth*,(Hunters Hill, Marist Fathers, 2010) pp143-156
48 Information from Archdiocese of Manila, Documentation Service, Vol XIII No.6 (June 2000)
49 Cardinal Joseph Ratzinger, Theological Commentary to Secret of Fatima, Documentation Service, P. 21
50 Therese of Lisieux, *Her Last Conversations* (Washington: ICS, 1977) 17,7
51 Irenaeus, *Against Heresies*, 111, 22,4
52 *Lumen Gentium*, 61
53 Ibid. 62
54 ibid., 60
55 Ibid.
56 In this section the teaching is from John Paul II, *Redemptoris Mater*, 38-43
57 See Donald Calloway, *No Turning Back: a Witness to Mercy*, Marian Press, 2010. This story told by Sarah Chichester, A Mother's Faith, A Son's Conversion, website www.marian.org; Marian Fathers of the Immaculate Conceptions.

58 Ibid.

59 The details of this history are well known. A good introduction to the background to the historical connection between the Rosary and Mary Help of Christians, and this title for the patroness of Australia: Servants of Mary Help of Christians, Brief History of Devotion to Mary Help of Christians, Broadway: The Marian Centre, 2001.

60 The story was reported on Youtube by CatholicNewsagency, April 27, 2015

61 The story, A Former Satanist who became a Saint, can be found on website of Dominican Friars Foundation of New York: df@domincanfriars.org

62 *Rosarium Virginis*, 60-61

63 *Lumen Gentium* 53

64 St Augustine , Sermons, 267, 4

65 Ignatius of Latakia, The Uppsala Report, 1968, Geneva WCC, p.298

66 *Lumen Gentium* 58

67 For the early story see Mary Craig, *Spark from Heaven*, London: Hodder & Stoughton, 1988

68 This story together with others can be found in Christine Watkins, Of Men and Mary, *How Six Men Won the Greatest Battle of their Lives*, Sacramento California: Queen of Peace Media: 2018

69 Raniero Cantalamessa, Sober Intoxication of the Holy Spirit, (Cincinnati: Servant Books, 2005) pp 1-20

70 *Lumen Gentium*, 12

71 Pope John Paul II, Address to Ecclesial Movements and New Communities, 30th May 1998, St Peter's Square

72 Leon Joseph Cardinal Suenens, *A New Pentecost?*, (N.Y.: Seabury Press,1975) p.197

73 ibid., p.206

74 Pope John Paul II, *Redemptoris Mater*, 28
75 ibid.
76 Judy Landrieu Klein, *Mary's Way*, (Notre Dame Indiana, Ave Maria Press, 2016) pp.39-40
77 ibid., p.39
78 See Rev. Robert J. Billet CMF, St Catherine Laboure and he Miraculous Medal, at marys-touch.com. 2018
79 See Cedric Wright "Miracle on Death Row", AD2000, August 2014 p.13 and Catholic Family News in USA 2001 website
80 Story told in Paul Glynn, *Healing Fire from Frozen Earth*, (Hunters Hill: Marist Brothers books, 1999) pp.168-176
81 Story told, Paul Glynn, ibid., pp27-35
82 Pope Paul VI, *Evangelii Nuntiandi*, 75
83 For information see Franciscan Friars of the Immaculate, *A Handbook on Guadalupe*, Bedford MA: Academy of the Immaculate, 1996
84 ibid., p.145
85 John O'Connor MSC, Our Lady of Kurduntiga, in Annals Australia, January-February 1997, pp13-15.
86 As with the famous St Louis Marie Grignion de Montfort in *True Devotion to the Blessed Virgin Mary* and *The Secret of the Rosary*. He points out that our perfection depends on our consecration to Christ. Since Mary is the most conformed to Christ of all creatures, then consecration to her will mean consecration to Christ. I understand what this great saint means. But for me it is just a matter of appropriate language to stay with "entrustment to Mary". In effect it is the same reality.